CERTIFIED SAFE

The Basics of Food Safety
and Hygiene Practices to
Grow your Business

PAVITHRA KRISHNA PRASAD

INDIA · SINGAPORE · MALAYSIA

Notion Press

No. 8, 3rd Cross Street,
CIT Colony, Mylapore,
Chennai, Tamil Nadu – 600 004

First Published by Notion Press 2020
Copyright © Pavithra Krishna Prasad 2020
All Rights Reserved.

ISBN 978-1-64983-917-6

Contents

Foreword.. *5*

Acknowledgements *9*

Who is This Book For? *11*

How to Use This Book? *13*

Who Am I?.. *15*

1. **Introduction**..**17**

   1.1. What is Food Safety? 17

   1.2. The Role of FSSAI in Food Safety 17

   1.3. What is FSSAI's Role? 18

   1.4. Best Practices to Adopt When You Start a Small-Scale Food
        Business 18

   1.5. Food Business Operator (FBO) 20

   1.6. FSSAI Registration vs Licensing 20

   1.7. Steps Involved in Registering Your Business.............. 21

   1.8. FSSAI has Upgraded FLRS to FoSCoS...................... 23

   1.9. Strategy for Migrating from FLRS to FoSCoS 25

2. **Why Food Safety?**..**35**

3. **General Hygiene and Sanitary Practices for Food Entrepreneurs** 37

  3.1. Location and Surroundings 38

  3.2. Design and Facilities.. 39

  3.3. Water 42

  3.4. Waste Disposal and Drainage System 46

  3.5. Equipment, Vessels and Containers.................................... 48

  3.6. Personal Hygiene and Grooming.. 49

  3.7. Receiving and Purchasing.. 51

  3.8. Cleaning and Sanitation of the Produce/Raw Materials........... 53

  3.9. Storage 55

  3.10. Pre-Processing/Pre-Production 58

  3.11. Product/Process/Control of Operations and Service 61

  3.12. Packaging, Distribution and Transportation 66

  3.13. Takeaways/Delivery by a Third Party................................ 67

4. **Beware of the Hazards** 69

  4.1. Physical Contaminants.. 69

  4.2. Chemical Contaminants 71

  4.3. Biological Contaminants/Hazards 72

  4.4. Allergens 74

Frequently Asked Questions: General Hygiene and Sanitary Practices 77

Frequently Asked Questions: Cleaning and Sanitisation 85

Frequently Asked Questions: Control of Operations/Process 93

Frequently Asked Questions: Service, Distribution and Transportation .. 99

Frequently Asked Questions: Packaging and Labelling...................... 101

Frequently Asked Questions: Pest Control 107

Frequently Asked Questions: Cross-Contamination............................ 109

Frequently Asked Questions: Training and Awareness......................... 113

Glossary 117

Annexure 119

References.. 127

Foreword

I have known Pavithra as a student during her UG program and I am indeed proud that she has penned down all essentials pertaining to food safety in commercial kitchens which can be adapted by home chefs too.

The book has very lucidly detailed all information right from registering a business to customer handling in a food establishment. Details of training that food entrepreneurs would have to undergo and the basic knowledge of a good food has been detailed with clarity.

The FAQ format makes it an interesting read and helps in easy assimilation of the important facts.

– Dr. Usha Ravi, Food Scientist
Ex. HOD of Food Science Department
MOP Vaishnava College for Women

I have found the book to be very helpful for a start-up as well as the existing Restaurant owners

"Certified Safe" book has given more details about the food-safety standards that are needed for daily operations and it's a complete guide

Again, I would just like to express my heartfelt congratulations for creating this wonder which will help many food establishments.

I wish you all the best.

Manoharan Karthik
CEO, Rasavid Group of Restaurants

'Certified Safe' by Pavithra Krishna Prasad is a must read for entrepreneurs in the food space. Navigating through statutory guidelines and various food safety compliance sometimes can be mundane and challenging. The book makes it easy to understand and is very well structured. The recent launch of FoSCoS and associate procedures have been lucidly explained. Eligibility criteria, documentation, validity have been clearly explained. The FAQ format is especially helpful.

When a company is in the business of food it has direct consequences and hence 'food safety' is paramount and non-negotiable. 'Certified Safe' navigates through all parameters like hygiene of the premises & staff, water, utensils, procurement of raw materials, proper storage etc. and can be referred to as a rulebook.

The book also refers to safety precautions given the current situation in the wake of COViD-19

Namrata Sundaresan
Partner Kirke Cheese Pvt Ltd (Kase Chennai)

A great restaurant is a place where a confluence of aromas envelope the room buzzing with animated conversations and laughter, the kitchen however paint a very different story.

As a professional chef, operating and maintaining kitchens may be second nature but the chaos that accompanies it never ceases. Although a certain method to the madness is developed and perfected with years of practice, I've always felt the need for an authoritative yet easily comprehendible text for upcoming chefs to refer to in establishing essential kitchen protocols.

"Certified Safe" addresses this vacuum in literature by providing a comprehensive guide to personnel in the food industry to ensure they are in compliance with global best practices in maintaining their commercial kitchens while ushering a much needed culture of safety and hygiene, particularly in these unprecedented times where it's more necessary than ever.

Pavithra's research and approach in ensuring the sanctity of kitchens and their upkeep is pragmatic, easy to implement, exhaustive in its coverage and provides a strong foundation in understanding the importance of kitchen safety which is an invaluable tool to have for upcoming chefs.

I am certain this book will become essential reading for those operating commercial kitchens and with time elevates the standards of discourse on kitchen and safety protocols in the food & beverage industry.

Chef Mathangi Kumar
That Madras Place, Summer House Eatery
Noodl.madras, per se chennai, Patina-The Indian Diner

Acknowledgements

I dedicate this book to my grandparents, my parents and Kaushik.

I thank my mentor, *Pravin Shekar*, who has guided me throughout the process of writing this book and getting it published.

Special thanks to **Sushmita Vishwanathan** and **Arun Ramkumar** from **Mojo Canvas** for the brilliant cover design. Thanks also to my editor, **Ganesh Vancheeswaran.**

Who is This Book For?

This book is for the entrepreneurs entering the business of food preparation and supply. In other words, for those who are setting up a commercial eatery, catering unit, food truck, home kitchen and so on. The basics of food safety remain the same, regardless of the scale of the food business.

Indians have always loved to eat out: from street food to fine dining, we have always patronised various eating options because of the diversity of our food and preferences. But, due to the Covid-19 crisis, people are scared to eat food that has been prepared outside their home. Given consumers' panic, government authorities are giving more importance to food safety and hygiene standards. They are likely to implement these standards more strictly than ever before. In such a situation, it is important for you, as a food entrepreneur, to improve your hygiene and safety standards by at least a few notches. Only then will you gain the confidence of consumers, and be accepted by them.

Those who are new to the food industry may not know of all the procedures and regulations governing food safety and hygiene. It is likely that the authorities will levy much heftier penalties than before, on those who fail to adhere to the guidelines. Such failure will cost you not only money, but also reputation amidst consumers.

Which is why I wrote this book.

This book lists out simple steps and measures that you MUST take to be fully compliant with the standards and guidelines set by the government.

Adhering to these safety measures will increase the operational cost of your company, but only by a little. And if managed well, this is going to benefit you in the long term. You will not only avoid getting penalised by the government, but will also win the confidence of your customers. At a time when people are giving the highest priority to food safety and hygiene, they will recommend your business to others if they know that you are adhering to all the safety and hygiene standards at every step. And so, they will help increase your business.

In short, if you want to start your own small-scale food business, this book is an essential guide.

How to Use This Book?

The book has a few major topics. And under those major topics, it has several sub-topics. In addition, I have included Frequently Asked Questions (FAQs) that may arise in your mind. I have addressed all questions that may come up, clearly mentioning the steps and measures you need to take.

You can read this book from start to finish, or jump straight to the question to which you need an answer. I suggest you read the whole book first, to get a complete view of the subject.

If you are facing a question that has not been addressed in this book, please write to me at fsg@pavithrakrishnaprasad.com or reach out to me through my website www. pavithrakrishnaprasad.com.

Who Am I?

I am a Food Safety Specialist with the accreditations given below:

- Certified Hygiene Rating Auditor by FSSAI
- External Lead Auditor or FSSC22000:FSMS by BSI
- FSSAI's FoSTaC (Food Safety Training and Certification) Trainer of Trainers for:-

  - COVID-19 awareness
  - Advanced Catering and Manufacturing
  - Basic Catering
  - PCQI – Preventive Controls Qualified Individual

My specialisations include consulting, auditing and training. Helping food establishments meet food safety regulatory standards is my focus area. I guide food business operators (FBOs) at every step: from setting up the kitchen to getting accreditation from regulatory bodies. This helps them operate with peace of mind.

I aspire to drive efforts in food safety initiatives in society, and to reach out to as many people as possible. My YouTube channel, podcast, Facebook page and Instagram handle all go by the name **"Food Safety Genie".** Keep watching these for regular updates and advice.

www. pavithrakrishnaprasad. com

Introduction

1.1. What is Food Safety?

Before I venture to define the term "food safety", I would like to talk about the word **"food"** used in this term.

According to FSSAI, food is something - processed, semi-processed or raw-that is intended for human consumption.

"Food safety" refers to the practices adopted to keep food safe. It covers the methods, measurements and steps required to be followed in every process along the food chain (Receiving, Procuring, Handling, Storage, Processing, Transport and Distribution) to prevent food-borne illness.

1.2. The Role of FSSAI in Food Safety

There are several Acts and Orders (like the Prevention of Food Adulteration Act-1954, and the Milk and Milk Products Act-1992) that define the standards expected by the regulatory bodies. To bring clarity to the legislation and to the stakeholders involved, a single Act -The Food Safety Standards Act of 2006 - was passed on 23rd August 2006.

Accordingly, FSSAI, a statutory body, was established by the Ministry of Health and Family Welfare in September 2008. FSSAI's rules and regulations have been enforced from 5th August 2011.

1.3. What is FSSAI's Role?

FSSAI is a central regulatory body that lays down food standards based on science, promoting public health through the regulation and supervision of food safety. In other words, it establishes the standards and regulations for food safety in India.

The following are the aspects in which regulations have been laid down by FSSAI:

1. Licensing and registration
2. Food products standards and food additives
3. Food packaging and labelling
4. Laboratory and sampling analysis
5. Import and export
6. Alcoholic beverages
7. Fortification of food
8. Advertisement and claims
9. Guidelines for theaccreditation of laboratories for food testing
10. Harmonising the standards as per global norms, and contributing to their development
11. Co-ordination with the state food authorities
12. Promoting awareness about food and nutrition

1.4. Best Practices to Adopt When You Start a Small-Scale Food Business

If you have decided to start a food business, you must know the nature of the industry: the vertical categorisation and the product you are going to sell.

Identify the industry vertical to which your food business belongs

From the list given below, identify the vertical and the category of your food business:

1. Hotel
2. Fast-food restaurant
3. Cafe
4. Caterers - industrial and institutional
5. Sweet stall and bakery
6. Fine dining
7. Resto-bar
8. Quick service restaurant
9. Manufacturing unit
10. Retailer
11. Canteen/club
12. Slaughterhouse/meat processing unit
13. Hawker
14. Cloud kitchen
15. Cold storage unit
16. E-commerce

Next, identify the nature of your product:

1. Raw
2. Semi-processed
3. Organic
4. Fortified
5. Processed-handmade or machine-made
6. Packaged
7. Ready to eat
8. Ready to cook
9. Frozen
10. Dehydrated

Before I dive deeper, I will explain a few terms that are used in the forthcoming sections, so that you will understand them easily.

1.5. Food Business Operator (FBO)

An FBO is any person or entity carrying out activities like manufacturing, processing (this can be catering or other kinds of processing to increase the shelf-life of the product), storage, distribution, retailing, transportation, etc. pertaining to food products.

Petty Food Business Operator

Petty food business operators are:

1. Those petty retailers, hawkers, small vendors, temporary stallholders, street food vendors and food trucks, whose annual food business turnover is less than Rs. 12 lakhs.
2. Food operators having a production capacity that is less than 100kg/day.
3. Food operators with a production capacity of less than 500litres per day, in the case of milk or any other liquid.

The first step in any food business is to identify the product to be sold, the vertical and the scale of the business.

The next step pertains to registering and procuring a license for the food establishment.

1.6. FSSAI Registration vs Licensing

FSSAI Registration and Licensing are mandatory for starting any food business in India. As per Section 31 of the FSS Act-2006, no person shall commence or carry out any food business activity, except under a license or registration.

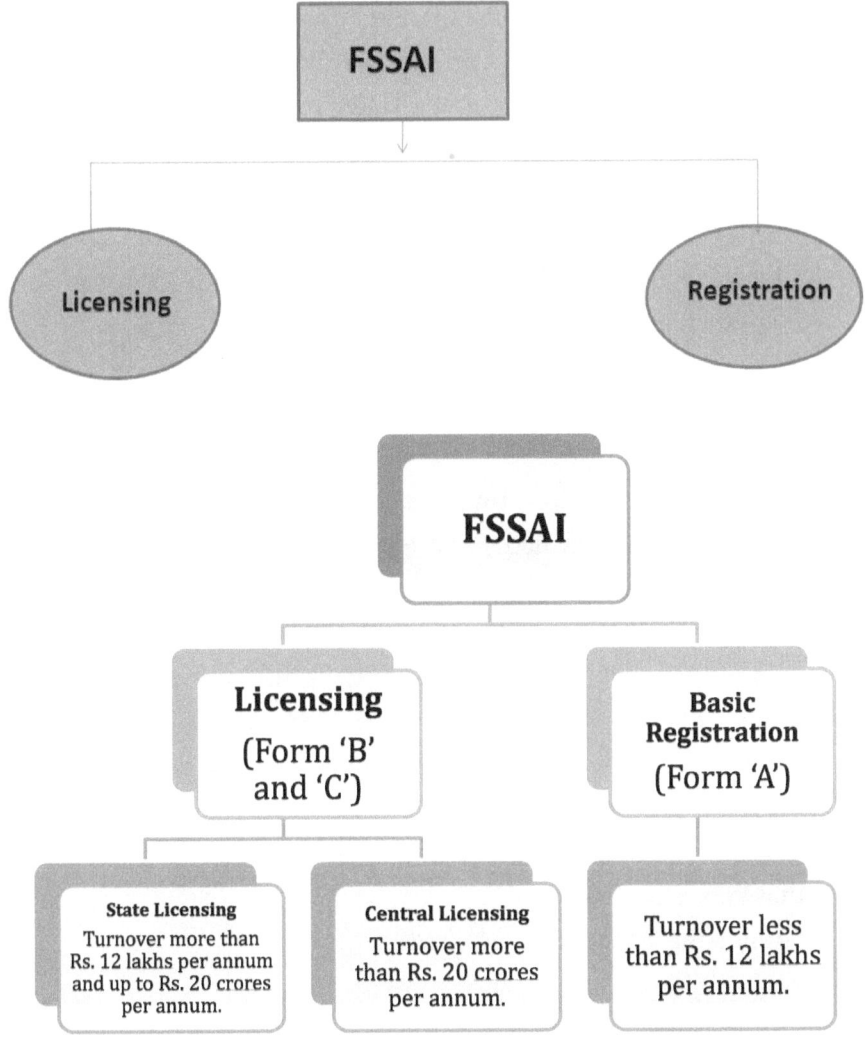

Since this book is for those who are planning to start a home-based/small-scale catering business, FSSAI Basic registration (FORM-A) is enough for the initial stages.

1.7. Steps Involved in Registering Your Business

1. Visit **www. fssai. gov. in**
2. Signup to create your login details.
3. You will land up on the "FBO signup" page.

4. Fill in all the mandatory details and create a user ID and password.

5. After completing the above step, in the right-hand side corner, you will see "existing new user". Enter your user ID and password here to log in.

6. Check for the eligibility criteria, and for the documents required- which are mandatory to be submitted.

7. Check for the kind of business, the criteria and the registration fee. The fee for basic registration is Rs. 100/-.

8. You can check the fee structure on the dashboard of the website.

9. After signing in, select from the toolbar the option "apply for license/registration".

10. Accept the declaration/undertaking.

11. Select the state in which you are applying for the registration.

12. Answer the first question (If the organisation is in more than one location- Yes/No).

13. Also answer this one: Are you applying for regional office/head office- Yes/No?

14. Next, you will be taken to a page containing the criteria. Choose the criteria for registration and other related criteria, if any.

15. Go back to the dashboard and click on the supporting documents that you may need.

16. Supporting documents required:

   - Photo of the FBO/applicant
   - ID proof, such as ration card, driving license, Aadhar card, PAN card details
   - Supporting documents (if any)- NOC by the Municipality or Panchayat, Health NOC.
   - Self-declaration.

17. Agree to the terms and conditions (if any).

Petty Food Business Operators (FBOs) do not need a license, as long as their business turnover per annum does not exceed Rs. 12 lakhs.

This book deals in detail with the FSSAI Registration and regulatory practices that must be followed by a small-scale or a basic caterer/food supplier.

1.8. FSSAI has Upgraded FLRS to FoSCoS

FoSCoS stands for Food Safety and Compliance System (FoSCoS). Since 2011, the FSSAI's online licensing platform FLRS (Food Licensing and Registration System) has been the soul of the licensing ecosystem, with 100 % pan-India coverage (including all states and Union Territories). FoSCoS replaces FLRS. Users from any state/UT are now required to visit https://foscos.fssai.gov. in and login using the same user id and password they are currently using on FLRS.

FoSCoS is a user-friendly website, and comes with an intuitively-designed homepage. It provides smart search options for license eligibility and the criteria for standardised products.

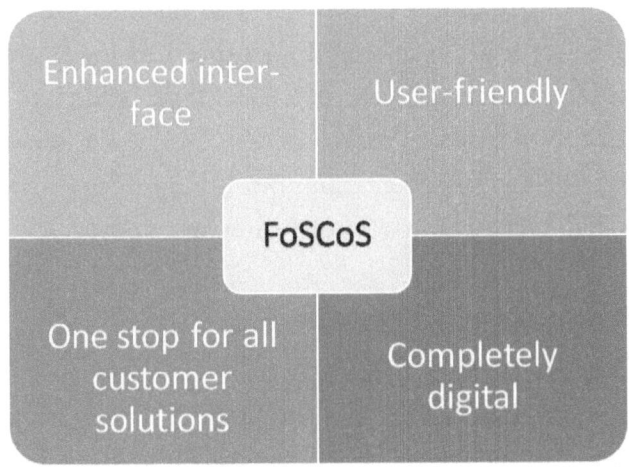

The concept of FoSCoS

FoSCoS has been conceptualised as a one-point stop for all the interactions of an FBO pertaining to regulatory compliance. FoSCoS has been integrated with the FoSCoRIS mobile app, and will soon be integrated with the IT platforms of FSSAI, such as INFOLNet,

FoSTaC, FICS, FPVIS, etc. Modules pertaining to sample management, improvement notices, adjudications, audit management systems, etc. will be enabled on this website in a phased manner in the future.

FoSCoS: only for manufacturers of standardised food products

Standardised Food Products are those that are defined under regulations; for example, fruit jam, fruit drinks, sauces, biscuits, carbonated water, etc.

Non-Standardised Food Products, also known as proprietary Foods, are those which are not specified under regulations. These regulations lay down the procedure for the grant of prior approval of non-specified food and food ingredients. FBOs are required to submit the prescribed application form, along with the necessary documents and a fee, as specified by the Authority. Approval for these products is granted by the Authority after the risk analysis is carried out by the Scientific Panels.

FoSCoS' new approach is only for the manufacturers of standardised food products. For manufacturers of non-specified food, supplements/ nutraceuticals, proprietary food and substances added to food, the approach continues to be as mentioned in FLRS. For all other kinds of businesses, such as catering, transport, storage, etc. , the licensing/ registration shall be based on a "broad category" approach, as earlier.

Launch of FoSCoS and its working

1. FoSCoS shall be launched in phases.
2. Once it is launched in a state/UT, all licenses/ registrations pertaining to the state/UT will be available on FoSCoS, and the FLRS data shall be disabled for taking any action.
3. However, initially, users can view their issued licenses/registrations or under-process applications on FLRS also.
4. Users will not be required to immediately do anything upon migration to FoSCoS, other than verify the correctness of details in the issued licenses/registrations and under-process applications.

5. However, all manufacturers holding a valid FSSAI license will have to modify their license to FoSCoS before 31st December 2020, and choose from the available list of standardised products.

1.9. Strategy for Migrating from FLRS to FoSCoS

Users of the FSSAI licensing and registration system (primarily, food businesses and Licensing/Registering Authorities) are required to follow the steps described below, after the launch of (FoSCoS) in their State/ UT.

Please note: The user ids and passwords will remain the same in FoSCoS, as they were in FLRS.

1. Valid FSSAI Licensed food businesses (non-manufacturing business) or Registered food businesses (all kinds of businesses):

   a. Visit the FoSCoS website after it is launched in your state.
   b. Verify the details of your existing licenses/registration certificates (like License or Registration number, name and address of the food business, kind of business (KOB)enrolled, validity, etc.) on FoSCoS (https://foscos. fssai. gov. in).
   c. Until an announcement is made by FSSAI, FLRS will remain functional for viewing purposes, but no transaction will be allowed on it. Licensed or Registered food businesses can view the details of their existing license/registration on the FLRS site.
   d. Any anomaly in License/Registration details is to be brought to the notice of FSSAI.

2. Valid FSSAI Licensed food businesses (manufacturing business):

   a. Visit the FoSCoS website after it is launched in their state.
   b. Verify the details of your existing Licenses/Registration certificates (like License or Registration Number, name and address of the food business, kind of business enrolled, validity, etc.) on FoSCoS (https://foscos. fssai. gov. in).

c. Modify your license (without any cost) at the earliest by selecting the products being manufactured from the standardised list of products available in FoSCoS. In FLRS, there was a text box approach for writing the name of the products to be manufactured. But, in FoSCoS, a product selection-based methodology has been adopted to make it easier for food businesses to select standardised food products.

d. Until an announcement is made by FSSAI, FLRS will remain functional for viewing purposes, but no transactions will be allowed on it. Licensed or Registered food businesses can view the details of their existing License/Registration on FLRS.

e. FoSCoS allows specific documents to be uploaded online, instead of all the documents shown earlier on the FLRS portal. Several declaration-based documents have been converted to checklists and tick-based declarations.

f. The whole process of FoSCoS is yet to be explained clearly by the regulatory bodies. But, the shift from FLRS will soon happen, and FoSCoS will be the portal for access to every detail about Food Business Operators.

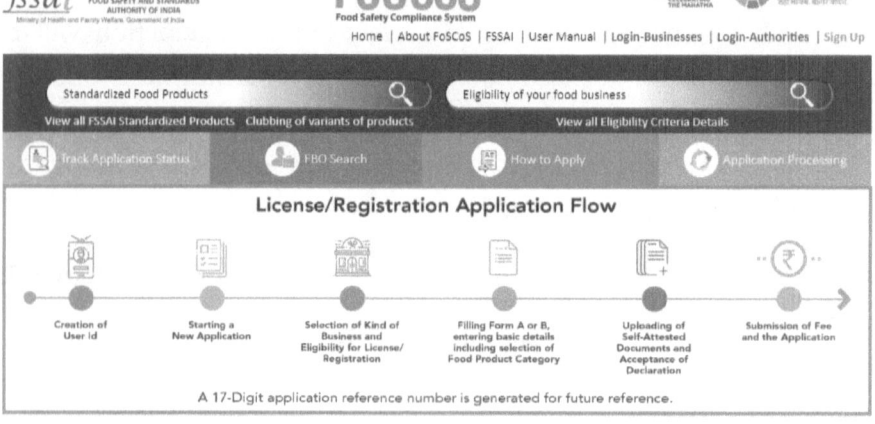

FREQUENTLY ASKED QUESTIONS

Licensing and Registration

What are the eligibility criteria for Registration and Licensing?

Eligibility criteria for FSSAI Registration

Petty FBOs are eligible to apply for FSSAI registration. These include:

- Those who manufacture or sell food items, either by themselves or via a retailer, hawker, itinerant vendor or a temporary stall owner.
- Those who distribute food. This includes distributors of food at any religious or social gathering, except caterers.
- Other food businesses, including small scale or cottage industries and such other industries relating to the food business, or tiny food businesses with an annual turnover not exceeding Rs. 12 lakhs and those whose production capacity of food other than milk and milk products, and meat and meat products, does not exceed 100 kg or litres per day, as applicable.
- Those businesses whose procurement or handling and collection of milk is up to 500 litres of milk per day or up to 2. 5 metric tons (MT) of milk solids per annum.

- Vegetable oil processing units, including units that are producing vegetable oil by the process of solvent extraction, and refineries -including oil expeller units with a turnover of up to 100 kg or litres per day, as applicable.
- Meat processing units with a production of more than 100 kgs per day or 30 MT per day, or whose slaughtering capacity is 2 large animals or 10 small animals or 50 poultry birds per day or less.
- All food processing units, other than those mentioned above, including re-packers with a capacity of up to 100 litres or kg per day.
- Cold storages, including the Storage Excluding Controlled Atmosphere Cold, as well as cold and refrigerated storages, and cold storages which are temperature-controlled, each having a turnover of up to Rs. 12 lakhs per annum.
- Wholesalers, retailers, distributors and suppliers having an annual turnover of upto Rs. 12 lakhs.
- Dhaba owners and other food vending establishments, along with clubs and canteens having a turnover of upto Rs. 12 lakhs per annum.
- Hotels and restaurants with a turnover of upto Rs. 12 lakhs per annum.
- Transporters with an annual turnover of upto Rs. 12 lakhs.

Eligibility criteria for FSSAI Licensing

A licence is for FBOs that do not classify as petty food businesses. Often, the amount of business FBOs do, in terms of income and yearly production capacity, makes them eligible for a licence. The FSSAI Licence is of two types: a State FSSAI Licence and Central FSSAI Licence.

You have to take a **State FSSAI Licence**if you belong to any one of the following types:

- Dairy units, including milk chilling units that are equipped to handle or process milk from 501 litres per day (LPD) to 50, 000 LPD or 2. 5 million tons (MT) to 2, 500 MT of milk solids per annum.
- Vegetable oil processing units and refineries involved in the process of solvent extraction, which include oil expeller units that produce up to 2 MT per day or have an annual turnover of Rs. 12 lakhs and above.
- Slaughtering units that have a capacity of between 2and 50 large animals, between10 and 150 small animals or between 50 and 1000 poultry birds per day.
- Meat processing units that have a capacity of up to 500 kg of meat per day or 150 MT per annum.
- All food processing units, including re-labellers and re-packers with a capacity of more than 100 kg and up to 2 MT per day. This includes all grain, pulse and cereal milling units.
- Storage businesses, excluding those which have controlled atmosphere and cold, with a capacity of upto 50, 000 MT per month.
- Storages that are cold and refrigerated, with a capacity of more than 10, 000 MT per month.
- Storages that are cold *and* controlled atmosphere with a capacity of more than 10, 000 MT per month.
- Wholesalers who have an annual turnover of up to Rs. 30 crores.
- Retailers, distributors, suppliers and caterers with a turnover of upto Rs. 20 crores per annum.
- Dhaba owners, or owners of other food vending establishments, as well as clubs and canteens that have an annual turnover of Rs. 12 lakhs.
- Hotels that have a rating of between 3-star and 5-star.
- Restaurants with a turnover of upto Rs. 20 crores per annum.
- Marketers with a turnover of upto Rs. 20 crores per annum.

- Transporters with a minimum of 100 vehicles or wagons, or an annual turnover of upto Rs. 30 crores per annum.

The eligibility criteria for FBOs to apply for a **Central FSSAI Licence** include:

- Dairy units, including milk chilling units that are equipped to handle or process more than 50, 000 litres of liquid milk per day or 2500 MT of milk solids per annum.
- Vegetable oil processing units, including units producing vegetable oil by the process of solvent extraction, and refineries (including oil expeller units) that have a processing capacity of more than 2 MT per day.
- Slaughtering units which handle more than 50 large animals or 150 small animals or more than 1000 poultry birds per day.
- Meat processing units that process more than 500 kg of meat per day or 150 MT per annum.
- All food processing units (including re-labellers and re-packers) that are processing more than 2 MT per day, except grain, cereal and pulse milling units.
- All manufacturers of proprietary foods.
- All 100% export-oriented units.
- All importers who are importing food items (including food ingredients and additives) for commercial use.
- Storage units, other than those having controlled atmosphere and cold environment, with a capacity of more than 50, 000 MT per annum.
- Cold or refrigerated storage units having a capacity of more than 10, 000 MT per annum, and controlled atmosphere + cold storages having a capacity of more than 1, 000 MT per day.
- Wholesalers having a turnover of more than Rs. 30 crores per annum.

- Retailers, distributors, suppliers and caterers having an annual turnover of more than Rs. 20 crores.
- Hotels that have five-star rating and above.
- Restaurants having a turnover of more than Rs. 20 crores per annum.
- Transporters having more than 100 vehicles or a turnover of more than Rs. 30 crores per annum.

What are the documents required when applying for an FSSAI Registration?

a. Application in Schedule-1
b. A fee of Rs. 100/- per annum
c. Address proof (a government document, like Voter ID card)
d. Photograph of the applicant

The Registration Card should be exhibited at a prominent place of your business premises.

What is the validity of the FSSAI registration?

It ranges between 1 year and 5 years (depending on the option you choose) from the date of issue of the registration number, subject to the remittance of the fee applicable for the period and compliance with all the conditions.

How will I know the date of expiry/renewal?

You will be notified 120 days before the renewal or expiry date. Any renewal must be made 30 days prior to the expiry date indicated in the certificate. If renewed within less than 30 days, before the expiry date, a late fee of Rs. 100/- per day of delay will be incurred.

I have applied for registration, but haven't got any confirmation. What should I do?

The Registering Authority shall consider your application, and may either grant permission or reject it with reasons which are recorded in writing; or issue a notice for inspection within 7 days of receipt of your application for Registration.

In the event of an inspection by the Food Safety Officer, the Registration shall be granted by the Registering Authority after being convinced of the safety, hygiene and sanitary conditions of the premises, within a period of 30 days.

If the Registration is not granted, or the inspection order is not received within 7 days, or no such communication is received within 30 days, you may start your business, provided the establishment and the business complies with any improvements suggested by the Registering Authority on a later date.

I have received confirmation of the FSSAI Registration. What should I do?

The Registering Authority will issue the registration certificate along with the date of validity, expiry date, your photo identity, the certificate number and the nature of your food business. You will have to display this at all times at a prominent place within the premises/cart/vending machine/kiosk/ wherever your business is located.

You will also have to bear in mind that the Registering Authority may conduct a surprise food inspection at any instance. This will be carried out by a Food Safety Officer.

I'm conducting a home business activity for self-help groups or NGOs which are Government-registered. Do I need to obtain an FSSAI Registration for this?

You must be a registered member of a society which is Licensed/ Registered with FSSAI and subject to all conditions, as laid down in the order.

I have closed down the business. How should I surrender the registration or license?

You need to surrender your Registration/License application by logging into the FLRS/FoSCoS account. After the approval of the concerned authority, your registration /license will be considered suspended.

Do I need to submit the annual returns of my business every year?

No, you don't have to. Only with those with a turnover of more than Rs. 12 lakhs per annum shall be required to submit annual returns.

Do I have to obtain a Registration or License for my vehicle, which is used for food distribution?

This is not applicable for basic catering outfits, whose turnover is below Rs. 12 lakhs per annum. It is applicable to those FBOs having a number of specialised milk tankers, refrigerated or insulated vans, etc.

What is the Food Products Standards and Food Additives Regulation Act, 2011?

This Act deals with the implementation of various standards of the foods contained therein. It provides detailed standards of various food products and food groups, laying down microbiological and additives requirements for different foods.

As an FBO, you should comply with the standards laid down for the food products for which you have been granted Registration/License.

The Food Products Standards and Food Additives Regulation Act, 2011 covers the following:

2. 1. Dairy products and analysis

2. 2. Fats, oils and fat emulsions

2. 3. Fruit and vegetable products

2. 4. Cereals and cereal products

2. 5. Meat and meat products

2. 6. Fish and fish products

2. 7. Sweets and confectionery

2. 8. Sweetening agents including honey

2. 9. Salt, spices, condiments and related products

2. 10. Beverages (other than dairy, fruits and vegetables)

2. 11. Other food products and ingredients

2. 12. Proprietary foods

2. 13. Radiation processing of food

2. 14. Gluten-free food

3. 1. Food additives

Appendix A: Food category system

Appendix B: Microbiological requirements

Why Food Safety?

To state the obvious, it's not an easy job to start a food business. This is because food businesses are vulnerable to human errors.

Food businesses following the best hygiene practices improve the quality of the process. As a direct consequence, the confidence level of customers in their business goes up. Since food is something that people consume, it is necessary to be extra-cautious about all aspects of its safety. Also, if you serve safe food under hygienic conditions, your customers will spread the word, thereby helping you get more customers. So food safety is vital for the health and expansion of your enterprise.

Food safety practices prevent food-borne illnesses and food spoilage during the process. Food-borne illnesses or diseases are caused by the consumption of contaminated or spoilt food. These are serious problems that affect public health. People with lower immunity- like children, elderly people and pregnant women- are more prone to food-borne diseases.

Your food establishment and all its food handlers should be cautious, and should follow the necessary practices to prevent food spoilage. Thereby, they should safeguard consumers from food-borne illnesses.

3

General Hygiene and Sanitary Practices for Food Entrepreneurs

These are the general hygiene and sanitary practices to be followed by food business operators/manufacturers/processors/handlers, applying for Registration.

Food safety covers not only food articles, but also other processes involved in the business: such as the surroundings, the premises and the actual facility, which are crucial parts of the definition of hygiene conditions.

A kitchen located next to a garbage dump, or a factory spewing chemical effluents will damage your efforts to maintain a hygienic kitchen.

If the kitchen lacks adequate ventilation and lighting, it can increase the chances of food spoilage. Also, do not forget the three kinds of hazards: physical, chemical and biological - which could cause severe food poisoning and food-borne illnesses.

Next, we look at a few essential tenets you must adhere to, in setting up a kitchen or any small-scale food business.

Here are a few basic hygiene and sanitary practices that must be followed by Petty FBOs and small-scale food businesses:

3.1. Location and Surroundings

- The location of the premises must be free from pollution and other bad elements that can harm the food.
- The premises must be located in a clean and hygienic environment.

- The premises must have adequate space and utilities for receiving, storing, pre-processing, processing, distributing and transporting the products.
- Separate each of the above-mentioned areas for easy identification, and to avoid confusion during the movement of goods.
- Avoid systemic contamination by not allowing other activities in the designated areas. A systemic contamination is that which occurs when activities takes place, deviating from the originally-drawn safety plans. For instance, systemic contamination occurs when activities that should actually take place in the receiving area happen in the kitchen, instead.

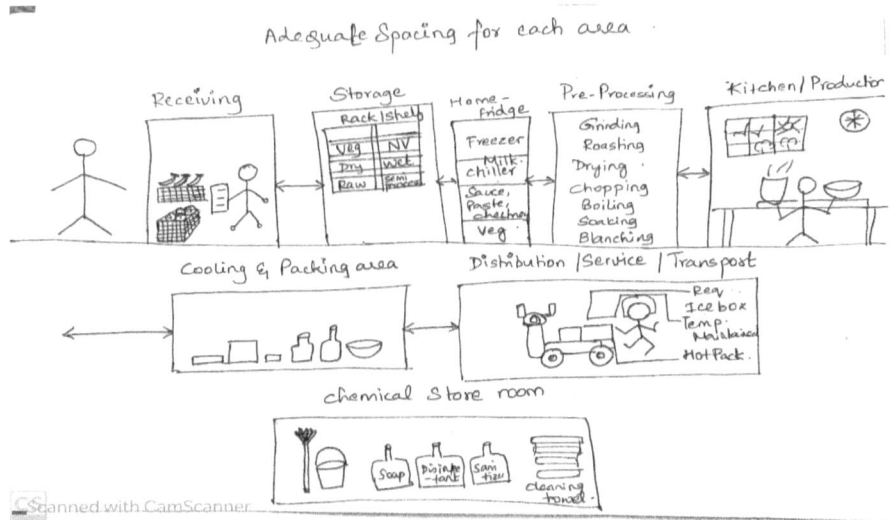

3.2. Design and Facilities

- The premises must be clean and ventilated with enough lighting, and have enough space for the movement and storage of goods.

- Air quality and ventilation system shall be designed and constructed in such a way that the air flow does not flow from contaminated areas to clean areas. The exhaust system to be effective in the kitchen for good air-flow process.

- An increase in humidity level (through, say, insufficient ventilation or exhaust) can increase the chance of the food getting spoilt.

- Lighting should be sufficient. The lighting fixtures should be covered and shatterproof to prevent breakages of electrical fitting to contaminate the food.

- If there is enough lighting, you will be able to clearly see the workers involved in any activity. Also, working in dim light increases the risks of not noticing dirt and other hazards, leading to unhealthy work conditions.

- If there is a free space for movement, the cleaning process will be easier and better.

Example of a kitchen with adequate spacing, lighting and ventilation

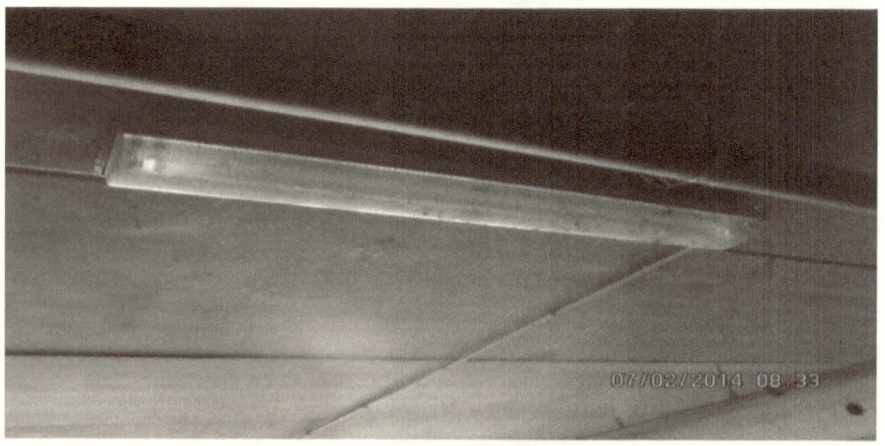

Example of insufficient lighting

- The floor, wall, and ceiling must be free from debris, gaps and flakes of paints.
- There should be smooth and easy access to all the structures, so that they can be cleaned properly.
- If these conditions are not met, the premises can become a breeding ground for pests and insects, apart from accumulating dirt and dust.
- The floor must be non-absorbent to dirt. Also, it should be moisture-free. Moisture can lead to the growth of mold and fungus.

- The doors and shelves must be smooth, and must not be a source of dirt, dust and pests.

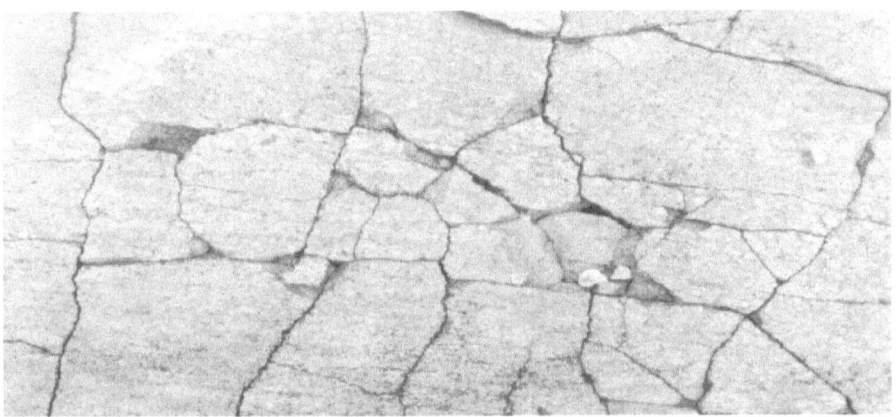

Example of a cracked floor that can attract dust and pests

Example of a non-absorbent floor with no gaps

- The facilities are to be deep-cleaned once a month to avoid the growth of mold and fungus. After cleaning, ensure that wet areas dry quickly. Regular cleaning (as opposed to deep cleaning) must take place every day.

- Ceilings face a major problem in winter. They absorb moisture, and have an increased tendency towards mold growth. Watch out for this.
- All nooks and corners must be regularly cleaned, to avoid an accumulation of cobwebs and dirt.

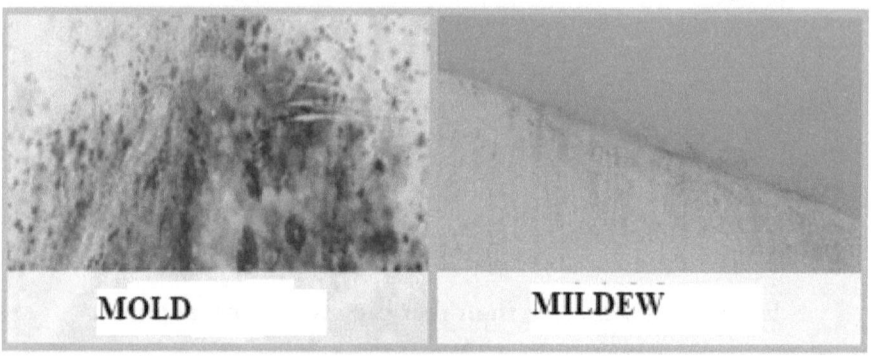

MOLD **MILDEW**

Example of mold growth on a wet ceiling

3.3. Water

- The water must be potable, and in continuous supply.
- Water pipelines must not be a source of contamination. The closed exterior is to be non-absorbent to moisture and dirt.
- Identify separate accesses for cleaning water and drinking water.
- Ensure that the water tank is cleaned once in 6 months.
- Water treatment has to be categorised as "water for non-food application", "food area washing application" and "food handling application, including guest drinking water".
- Water lines must run parallel to sewage lines.
- The lid of the storage tanks must be very tight, and capable of taking high loads. They should be repaired or replaced if there is any damage.
- There should be provision for hot and cold water for cleaning utensils/ equipment. It is recommended to follow three-sink methods for wash, rinse and sanitise the equipment & container. The containers and equipment must be air-dried for effective drying.

- Ice and steam for use in preparation of food shall be made of potable water. They should be handled hygienically to avoid cross-contamination. Handling ice can be via a scoop.
- Water should be tested bi-annually for IS10500 parameters. This is to check the potability of the water- chemically and microbiologically.
- Basic testing of water can be carried out on a monthly basis.

3.3.1. Contamination of water

Water that has been freshly contaminated, or possesses a continuous source of pathogens, is very harmful to health. Natural waters have a capacity to assimilate and transport waste. But, heavy water pollution has made self-purification a difficult process.

Water can get contaminated:-

1. At the source.
2. By addition of impurities during transit from source to reservoir.
3. During distribution, through lead pipes conveying water or through cracks and joints in the piping. Water pipes must always be at a safe distance from sewage and gas pipes.
4. When water is stored in underground or overhead tanks that is unclean.
5. When innumerable or unclean containers are dipped in the water container.
6. If unclean glasses are used to serve water or by faulty methods of holding the glasses.
7. Non-potable water can contaminate dishes, vegetables, etc. Ice made from contaminated water may render cold drinks unhealthy.

3.3.2. Hardness of water

- Water is considered hard when soap does not lather easily. The hardness is caused by compounds like calcium and magnesium dissolved in it. Water is considered soft when soap lather lasts for at least five minutes.

- Hardness in water is expressed in terms of mill equivalents per litre (mEq/l).
- In the catering and hospitality industries, the type of water used directly affects food service, preparation, dishwashing, laundry and the maintenance departments.
- Water used for consumption should be moderately hard. However, if hardness exceeds 3mEq/l, then water softening is recommended.
- Hence, softener water and soft water is used for laundry and dishwashing as they require heavy lather formation.

3.3.3. Basic steps involved in water purification

- **Ion exchange**

This is the first step of the purification process. The water from your city council is contaminated with unwanted minerals. This step, therefore, aids in removing the minerals that form hard water. Alum and other chemicals are added to the water and flocs (a loosely clumped mass of particles) are formed. The dirt particles are then attracted to the flocs, which then compel them to go down and settle at the bottom of the tank.

- **Sedimentation**

After the first step, the flocs and the water go through the sedimentation process. When the water settles, floc moves to the bottom and settles there. There are also sediment filters that trap dirt particles. This helps prevent the equipment from being polluted.

- **Sand filters and activated carbon filters**

Water is filtered and passed through layers of sand, charcoal and the rest. The particles that were left after sedimentation are then removed. A carbon filtration process is also involved, by which herbicides, chlorine and other pollutants are eliminated. The filter captures the impurities in the water.

- **Disinfection**

Water is moved to a closed tank that has ultraviolet light. Ultraviolet light is a sterilising agent. If it is underground water, this step is enough to sufficiently clean the water, because all the micro-organisms will be killed. After disinfecting the water, it flows through the pipes and processed through reverse osmosis.

- **Reverse Osmosis (RO)**

When the water reaches homes, it has to undergo another purification step called reverse osmosis. Here, a semi-permeable membrane is used to remove any impurities present in the water. All the dissolved contaminants that might have been missed in the previous stages of purification are removed now.

Disadvantages of RO

There are many who think that having an RO system simplifies the process of purifying water. But few are aware that this removes the beneficial minerals also from the water. The reverse osmosis process removes 92%- 99% beneficial calcium and magnesium.

Since this does not have many beneficial minerals, they leach minerals from the body, too. This means that the minerals and vitamins being present in food are taken away even before the food is consumed.

Also, studies state that to produce RO water, the machines have to expel 4 to 8 times the amount of waste as they do potable water. This comes to nearly 60 litres.

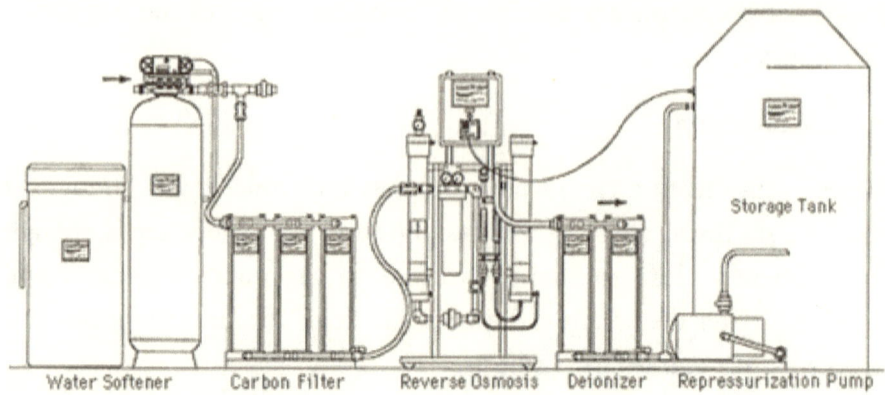

Water Softener   Carbon Filter   Reverse Osmosis   Deionizer   Repressurization Pump

Small-Scale purification

Boiling: Water must be boiled thoroughly at 100°C. This kills all spores and cysts, and yields sterilised water. Also, this removes temporary hardness of water. The disadvantage of boiling is that the organisms may re-contaminate upon cross-contamination.

3.4. Waste Disposal and Drainage System

Proper waste disposal and drainage system is to be followed.

- Segregate wet and dry waste to prevent pests from breeding.
- Place waste bins away from the kitchen.
- Clean and sanitise the waste bins on a regular basis.
- Use pedal-operated bins to avoid hands coming in direct contact with the bins.
- Do not discard any solid particles in your sink, as they tend to clog the sink and block the drainage.
- The drainage must be a minimum of 6 inches deep.
- The drain must flow opposite to the direction of food flow, from the service area to the receiving area.
- The drain should be free from clogging, back flow and stagnation.

- No drain should be open. Drains must always be grilled and closed to prevent pest-entry and breeding. Also, to prevent spreading of foul smell.
- The drain depth must be shallow at least 4 inches deep and must be perforated.
- A cockroach trap and pre-filters are to be placed in the drainage, to trap German cockroaches, and prevent them from entering through the drainage pipes.

Over-dumping and leaking

Examples of wet waste: vegetable and fruit peels, food waste and newspapers.

Example of dry waste: plastic, cardboard, electronic items, etc.

3.5. Equipment, Vessels and Containers

- Ensure that the equipment, vessels and containers used are of Food-grade material, which is safe for cooking and consumption.
- The most preferable material for this is stainless steel, which does not erode, rust or get contaminated.
- Your equipment, vessels, and containers must permit easy cleaning and placement.
- Ensure that these aren't made of copper, brass, lead, cadmium or zinc. These metals rust and corrode easily.
- Clean, wash, sanitise and dry these after every use.
- Place them away from the walls to prevent infestation, and to give easy access for cleaning.

Non-food grade materials like cadmium, brass and copper, when heated, these materials rust and corrode.

Stainless steel "food grade" vessels

3.6. Personal Hygiene and Grooming

- Your staff must wash and sanitise their hands and legs (using a 70% alcohol solution) before entering the premises.
- The requirements for hand washing and drying must include:-

  - Stainless steel/ Porcelain wash basin (preferable knee operated- to avoid direct contact and contamination)
  - Hand wash liquid soap (Germicidal)
  - sanitiser
  - provision and supply of hot and cold water
  - air-drying machine or a tissue roll
  - dust bin to discard wastes (preferably covered and pedal operated)

- Staff must wash their hands with soap and water for at least 20 seconds.
- Staff must wash and sanitise their hands:

  - after coughing or sneezing,
  - after using the toilet,
  - after handling raw food and before handling the cooking,
  - after touching any dirty surface or material,

- after touching any pet,
- after coming in contact with any high-touch point (like handles, chair, switchboards, etc.), and
- after touching their face, hair, or any other part of their body, and after handling any chemical.

- Staff must enter the kitchen only after a bath, and must use clean aprons, hand gloves (when required) and headgear during the process.
- They must follow proper grooming standards, such as having trimmed nails, shaved beard and short hair. Also, a no-jewel policy is to be followed in the kitchen.
- Any person with any sickness must stay away from the entire process. Any injury or wound must be properly covered at all times, and must not come in contact with the food.
- In light of the recent COVID-19 pandemic, it is advised that you check the temperature of the staff regularly, and before they enter the (temperature should not be above 98.6 F).
- Staff must wear face masks and gloves during the process. These are to be removed and disposed of after every use. Do not wear masks that have been used for more than 6 hours.
- Gloves must be worn while handling raw, unprocessed food.
- Prohibit eating, chewing, smoking and spitting in the kitchen.
- Ensure that a safe distance of 1 metre is maintained between any two staff members.
- Personal hygiene and grooming must be followed by all the staff, including the house-keeping and delivery staff.
- Staff working in wet areas (for instance, washing and cleaning vessels) have to wear disposable gloves, along with a coat.
- The restroom and lavatories shall be separate from food process and service areas to avoid staff having their food in restroom.

3.7. Receiving and Purchasing

- Close the area at all times. Open only when receiving produce.
- Regularly clean and sanitise the areas before and after receiving products.
- Ensure that there is a pest electric device/insectocutor/insect light trap that can reduce pests and flies. This should be installed 5 feet above the ground.
- Ensure that your suppliers maintain proper hygiene and grooming standards.
- Ensure that the suppliers are all approved by FSSAI. Check for their license, have a copy of it, and document it.
- Document the supplier invoices, FORM "C" (supplier's license) and FORM "E" (given on the next page) - a form of guarantee from the supplier- on a regular basis. This form will hold vendors responsible in case of any mishap.
- Document the supplier's COA (Certificate of Analysis) of their products supplied at least once in 6 months.
- Verify the product or the ingredients by properly following the "sort, grade and reject" technique. Check by weight, colour and physical characteristics of the product.
- Wear gloves and masks while inspecting items.

- Accept any product only after a proper inspection of raw material specifications. Check for the freshness, colour, weight, physical characteristics and visible contaminants.
- Do not receive non-vegetarian items in an open condition, as they are more susceptible to contamination.
- It is preferable to follow a "receiving time-table" every week to prevent receiving non-vegetarian and vegetarian items together.
- Care should be taken to clean, separate and wash all the received items in such a manner that dirt, grease, slush or other foreign matter attached to the surface of the food doesn't go beyond the receiving area.
- Due to COVID-19, it is advisable to use your own sanitised crates (especially for eggs) while receiving them.
- Remove all the tertiary and secondary packaging at the entry point itself. Tertiary packaging includes the carton, cardboard or any thermos foam packaging used for bulk handling. Secondary packaging includes the wrappers that are used for labelling products. Unlike primary packaging, this is not in direct contact with the product.
- The condition of the package shall be checked. Avoid receiving dented cans or puffed tetra packs, as they are not consumable. They are likely to be already spoilt.
- Check the label while receiving. Check the date of manufacturing or processing, and the validity/expiry date.
- Buy products only as per your requirement and storage capacity to avoid food spoilage and waste.

FORM E
Form of Guarantee
(Refer Regulation 2.1.14(2))

Invoice No. _____

From: _____

To: _____

Place: _____
Date: _____

Date of sale Nature and quality of article/brand name, if any		Batch No or Code No.	Quantity
Price			
1	2	3	4	5

I/We hereby certify that food/foods mentioned in this invoice is/are warranted to be of the nature and quality which it/these purports/purported to be.

Signature of the manufacturer/Distributor/Dealer

Name and address of

Manufacturer/Packer

(In case of packed article)

License No. (wherever applicable)

Image of Form "E"

3.8. Cleaning and Sanitation of the Produce/Raw Materials

- Wash all fruits and vegetables with lukewarm potable water.
- You can also sanitise them with 50 PPM chlorine/1% sodium hypochlorite- 4ml in 10litres of water. But washing and sanitising with lukewarm or saline water should be enough for a home-scale/small food business.
- Air-dry them thoroughly after washing.

- Vegetables can be sanitised by dipping them in saline water or a diluted solution of turmeric. Or, you could dip them in ice cold water and dry them thoroughly.
- Fruits sprayed with pesticides are to be soaked in saline water for an hour, and left to dry in a clean kitchen towel.
- Wash all the non-vegetarian produce with running water or hot saline water, but only prior to cooking.
- Wash eggs with 50 PPM chlorine- 4ml in 10 litres of water. You can also sanitise the eggs by soaking them in saline hot water and scrubbing them with a clean brush. Place them on a clean cloth, and dry them.

In short, follow this always: clean, dip, sanitise and dry.

Washing and Sanitisation of fruits and vegetables

1. Preparation and Cleaning	• Sanitise sink, vessels. Wash hands before coming contact with the produce. • Remove loose dirt and physical contaminants.
2. Sanitise	• Soak in hot water for 2-3 minutes. You can also wash these under running water. • You can use diluted saline, turmeric, vinegar to soak the vegetables. • Do not wash any root vegetables.
3. Rinse and Air-Dry	• Rub and rinse them. • Leave them to air-dry and then store.

- Drying the produce after sanitising it is an important step.
- Packed items like milk pouches, canisters, and cans are to be washed thoroughly before storing them in the refrigerator.
- Every carton, crate, tray and bottle received is to be sanitised and wiped thoroughly before storing it in the refrigerator.

3.9. Storage

- The store racks has to be stored away from the wall and a 2 feet above the floor, for easy access to cleaning.
- Raw food and cooked food are to be stored separately.
- Label the items with date tags for proper identification. The date tags must have the date of preparation and the "use by" date for easy identification.
- Milk is to be kept in the milk tray/chiller zone. Do not store any milk or milk products in the freezer. Conditions are different for ice creams.
- Store fruits and vegetables according to their needs (whether in the chiller or under ambient condition).
- Store potatoes, onions, sweet potatoes, unpeeled or uncut watermelons, mangoes, bananas, ginger and garlic under dry ambient conditions, and but not directly under the sun.
- Store meat and seafood in the freezer, at between -18°C and -22°C.
- Store pulses, lentils and grains dry.
- Shelves and containers must be clean and dry always.

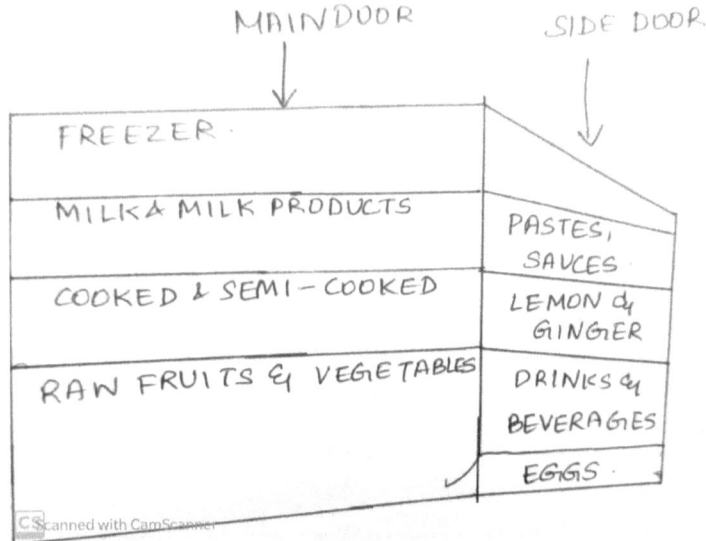

Storage practice to be followed in a refrigerator

- Do not use newspapers as a base for the kitchen shelves: they attract a lot of pests and dirt.
- No carton boxes to be kept in the kitchen; they absorb oily content, and in turn, attract more insects.
- Practise FIFO (First In First Out) or FEFO (First Expiry First Out). FEFO is to be followed for packaged, labelled items that have their shelf-life mentioned. On the other hand, FIFO is to be used for perishable items that don't have labels and are fresh-like fruits, vegetables, meat, seafood, etc. The stacking of the products must be such that the ones received first are to be used first. Keep track of the product's validity, and store it according to its expiry date.
- Do not overstock. Buy only what is needed. This way, you can reduce wastage.
- Store vegetarian and non-vegetarian foods separately. If possible, have a separate cooking space, separate containers and separate shelves for vegetarian and non-vegetarian food.
- No stacking or storing must lean on a wall; there should be a minimum gap of 10 inches.
- Store the products that have to be thawed on the lower rack to avoid dripping loss and contamination. In simple terms, thawing is defrosting; a slow process of ice or any other frozen substance becoming liquid or soft, so that it can be processed further. Thawing must be done either by "chiller thawing" (thawing overnight for at least 8 to12 hours under chiller conditions) or by "running water thawing" (placing the frozen product under running water at 15°C for 90 minutes).
- Do not store fruits or vegetables in plastic covers. Use clean cloth bags. Wash these cloth bags on rotation basis.
- Store chemicals separately. Label them clearly, and keep them away from the kitchen.
- Check the chiller temperature frequently. It should be between 0°C and 5°C.

- Date-tagging is a good method for tracking the product's validity. It's good to date-tag fresh items like vegetables and fruits for easier tracking of their date of receiving.

Storing dry products in a wet container leads to heavy mold and fungal growth

Carton boxes attracting German cockroaches in the kitchen

Newspapers absorb more oil. Also, its highly poisonous print sticks to the food product. Newspapers attract more pests and dirt, too.

Use of foils or paper to roll or pack food

There is a tendency to use foil to roll chappatis or other similar items. The use of only accredited foil and food grade butter paper is allowed for packing and rolling food items. Using wrong kind of paper or foil can pose chemical and biological hazards to the food.

3.10. Pre-Processing/Pre-Production

- This is the step prior to the production of food. In this, we clean, sanitise, chop, grind, dry, roast and knead the ingredients/raw materials.
- Always follow the 3-step process- clean, sanitise and dry- for proper cleaning and sanitisation.

1. Preparation and Cleaning	• Wash your hands before handling. • Remove dirt, loose items and any other physical contaminant.
2. Wash and Sanitise	• Sanitise with hot water (at 75 degree C) and detergent.
3. Air-dry	• Rub and rinse with clean potable water and a clean cloth. • Leave the equipmens to air-dry.

Cleaning and sanitisationmethod for food equipments and premises

- Other than the food produce, all the equipment and common touch-points like switchboards, doorknobs, glasses, and fridge knobs are also to be thoroughly sanitised frequently. It is preferable to so with a 70% alcohol solution.
- Clean the switch boards and electrical equipment only after switching off the electrical mains.
- There should be a schedule for cleaning all the equipment, storage area/shelves and the whole facility.

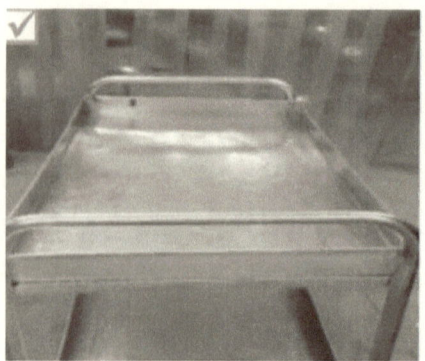

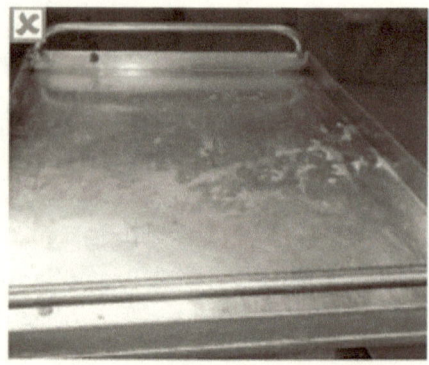

clean and sanitised tray for receiving raw materials

Unclean Trolley

- After every use, chopping boards are to be cleaned, sanitised and dried with hot salt water, diluted vinegar or even with water soaked with lime to avoid an increase in the count of micro-organisms breeding on these items. Chopping boards and knives can be sanitised with chlorine. In the case of vegetarian produce, use 50 PPM (4ml in 10 litres of water). For non-vegetarian produce, use 100 PPM (8ml in 10 litres of water).
- Use separate chopping boards and knives for vegetarian and non-vegetarian products. If possible, use colour-coded chopping boards for easy identification.
- Clean the kitchen counters, walls, equipment and wall corners regularly. You can follow the spray method by using 70% alcohol to sanitise the equipment, furniture, etc.
- Use separate towels for washing kitchen utensils and for wiping hands. Do not use cloth that has loose threads.
- Follow proper thawing/defrosting procedures for any frozen product. Use only potable water to thaw it. The flow is as follows: frozen products-chill them overnight-use them for cooking after they are thoroughly softened.
- Do not re-freeze anything. So, thaw only the required portion at a time.

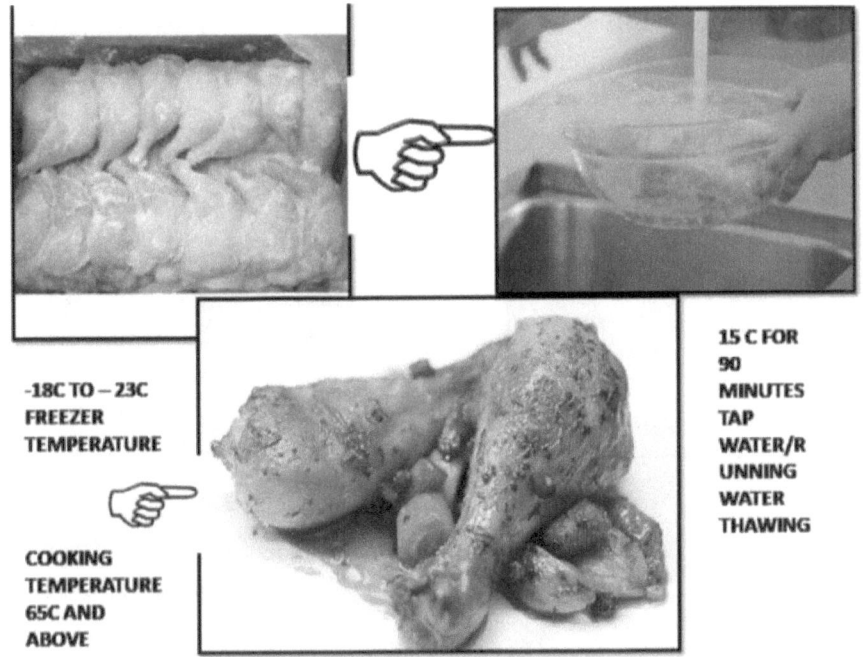

-18C TO – 23C
FREEZER
TEMPERATURE

15 C FOR
90
MINUTES
TAP
WATER/R
UNNING
WATER
THAWING

COOKING
TEMPERATURE
65C AND
ABOVE

Cold running water thawing procedure

3.11. Product/Process/Control of Operations and Service

- Cook the food at an optimal temperature of 65°C and above. Cooking above 65°C will kill the bacteria, unless the food is contaminated after cooking.
- For preparing of cold items like beverages, use potable water and sanitised fruits/vegetables.
- Use a thermometer for proper temperature reading.
- Ensure that salads, chutneys, paste and sauces are all stored in the chiller, and never at room temperature.
- Do not leave any processed food open. Cover them properly.
- Cooked foods are not to be left at room temperature. They should be served/consumed within 2. 5 hours of preparation, unless they are kept in a bain-marie or warmer condition (or in chiller condition, in the case of cold food). A bain-maire is anequipment with hot

water, where the cloches are placed for maintaining the temperature during serving/buffet.

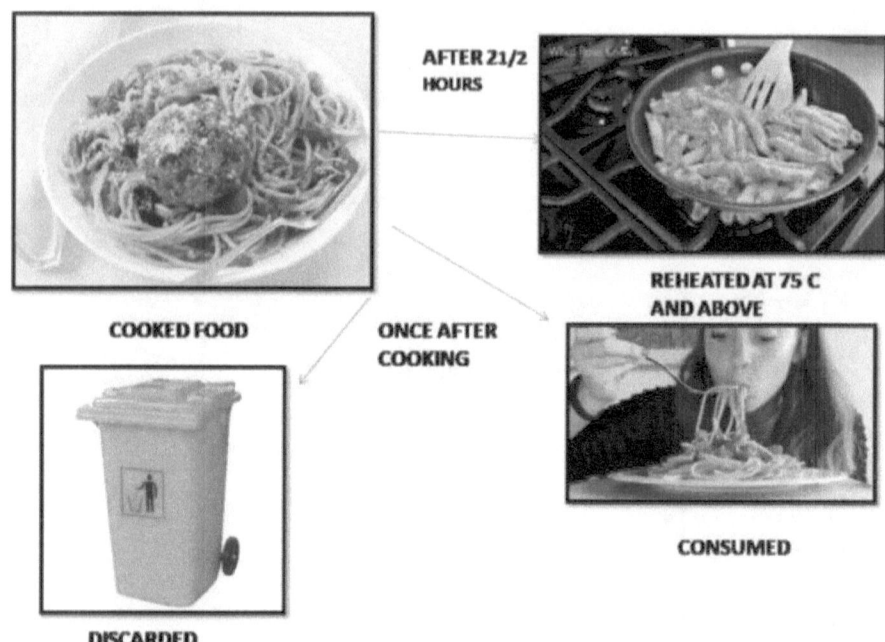

- Cooking oil is not to be used more than three times. Using the same batch of oil more than three times can lead to an increase in Total Polar Compounds (dark residues in oil). This results in the development of greyish smoke and foaming in oil. This leads to several diseases such as atherosclerosis, brain damage and even cancer.
- FSSAI has fixed a limit for Total Polar Compounds at 25 percent beyond which the vegetable oil shall not be used. You can test this via food testing labs.
- If you are selling a fried product, it's natural that the frequency of using cooking oil is higher. Change the oil for every batch. Using canola oil or sunflower oil is recommended, as they have higher smoking points.
- Smoking point, also known as flash point, is the temperature at which the oil stops shinning and starts giving out a lot of

smoke. This is the point at which the oil begins to oxidise (breakdown of Free Fatty Acids takes place). When oil begins to smoke, it imparts a burnt, bitter flavour to the food being fried. During this process, harmful compounds like Polar compounds are released as a by-product of the breakdown, as it is exposed to heat.

- Oils with a medium-smoke point, like groundnut/peanut oil, are suitable for greasing and pan-frying. "No-heat" oils, like walnut and flaxseed oil, are best for making dips and marinades.

- In general, the more refined the **oil**, the **higher** its **smoke point**, because refining removes impurities and free fatty acids that can cause the **oil** to **smoke**. Refined **oils** typically have a neutral taste and odour, and a clear appearance.

- Do not leave oil in direct sunlight. It can turn rancid and toxic. If you notice black sediments or blue-grey smoke, discard the oil; do not use it again.

- Leftover oil, and oil that has already gone bad, are to be separately collected in a container and sold to the aggregators. Do not discard them, as they possess highly reactive and toxic content.

- The aggregators collect oil to be used as bio-diesel, and for greasing machines.

Used Cooking Oil & TPCs

Total Polar Compounds are the non-volatile by-products (dark residues in oil) of repeated frying, which result in development of dark color and increased foaming in oil.

Image courtesy: fssai. gov. in

Indications that the quality of oil has deteriorated

Blue-grey smoke appears. Tough foam gets formed. Oil becomes dark and murky. The consistency of oil changes.

Image courtesy:fssai. gov. in

- **Wrong ways of re-heating food**

  - Adding water to the cooked content.
  - Heating on a bain-marie.

- **Correct ways of re-heating food**

  - Place the food in a pan, and heat it thoroughly till it reaches a temperature beyond 75°C at the core. The core temperature is found at the mid-point of the food, where the temperature is even.
  - Place food in an oven which is set to 165°C or more.

- Do not re-heat a product or cooked food more than twice. If you do so, you allow it to touch the "Danger Zone" Temperature is (5°C to 63°C). Danger-zone temperature is where the bacteria multiply rapidly. And so, it is always advisable to serve and consume hot food hot and cold food cold.

Food being heated by the addition of water

Do not reheat using a bain-marie

- Do not use food colours, unless it is for snack items and sweets (as the quantity of snacks and sweets we eat is supposed to be less than the quantity we eat of the main dishes).
- Use only approved colours; not those that are banned.

3.12. Packaging, Distribution and Transportation

- Sanitise delivery bags with 70% alcohol solution, and wipe them using non-absorbent material.
- Packaging material must be food-grade, tamper-proof and made of non-absorbent material (non-absorbent to water, oil and dirt).
- The container must be leak-proof and not brittle, so that it doesn't get damaged in transit.
- Transport vehicles must be serviced and kept clean.
- If the food is transported in a van or tempo, it is advisable to maintain the required temperature according to the nature of the food -either by providing an air-conditioner or by packing it in a hot pack.

A clean and sanitised delivery box

- Use a solid-freeze pack in the box to maintain cold temperatures during transit. For hot liquid food, use insulated thermo-flasks, while for solids, use insulated hot packs.
- Clean/sanitise the bike handles with a 70% alcohol solution after every delivery.

3.13. Takeaways/Delivery by a Third Party

- Due to Covid-19, it is best to maintain a safe physical distance in every activity.
- Only one staff member is to attend to the service.
- Staff must adhere to personal hygiene standards like wearing masks, head gears, aprons and gloves.
- Delivery staff should wait in the designated area only.
- The temperature of delivery agents should be checked. They must maintain good personal hygiene before and while handling the food.

- Delivery agents must wear gloves while handling packed food to avoid transmission of viruses.
- Your staff should leave the food outside your eatery, for the delivery staff to pick it up.
- All the surfaces should be cleaned and sanitised once an hour.

Beware of the Hazards

Hazards are those harmful and hazardous contaminants that can cause food-borne illnesses. These can be physical, chemical, biological contaminants and allergens.

4.1. Physical Contaminants

Any particle that can be easily picked up and sensed by touching is called a physical contaminant. These are contaminants that have found their way into the food - accidentally or through a deliberate act.

Examples: Hair strands, pins, staples pins, dust, plastic chips, insects, glass pieces, threads, etc.

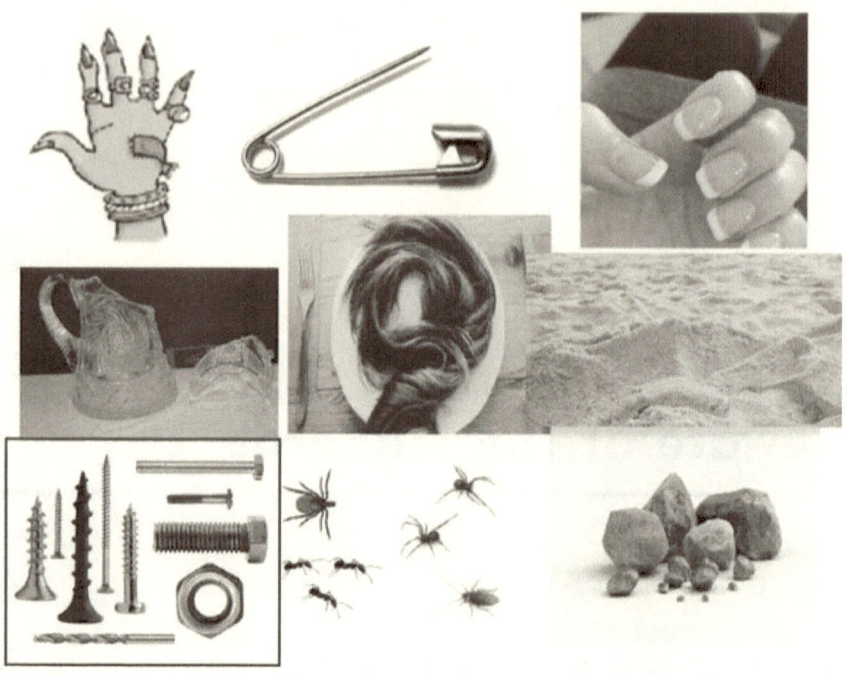

These, when consumed, can cause the effects of allergic and food poisoning on the body. A severe case of this is when the contaminants are consumed in a significant number or quantity.

4.1.1. How can physical contamination be prevented?

- Tie your hair and cover it with a proper head cap whenever you are cooking.
- Use shatter-proof covering on the exterior surfaces of lights to prevent them from breaking and falling into the food.
- Do not seal any open packet with stapler pins. They get rusted. Also, there is a high chance of their falling into the food.
- Do not use any rusted equipment/machine. Be sure to give all equipment/machines a coat of paint every three months. Even utensils and vessels rust if left unused for a long period. It is better to remove the rust using a paste made out of baking soda and water.

Use a brush with soft bristles to rub this paste onto the equipment, and clean the equipment thoroughly.

- Clear broken glass pieces and other materials, and take them away from the kitchen immediately.
- **Deep-clean the kitchen regularly.** Have a deep-cleaning schedule for the kitchen. During this process, corner of the walls, tile walls, fans, lights, exhaust fans, chimneys and all other not-easily-reachable points have to be cleaned thoroughly. Oil stains attract pests; also, they drip easily and fall into the food. Deep cleaning has to be done at least once a month. If the food production involves a lot of frying, then the kitchen has to be deep-cleaned every 15 days.

4.2. Chemical Contaminants

These are hazards from chemical products. These contaminants are not visible to the naked eye. The following are examples of sources of chemical contamination: pesticides, sanitising agents, cleaning agents, soap solutions, food colours, toxic metalsand preservatives.

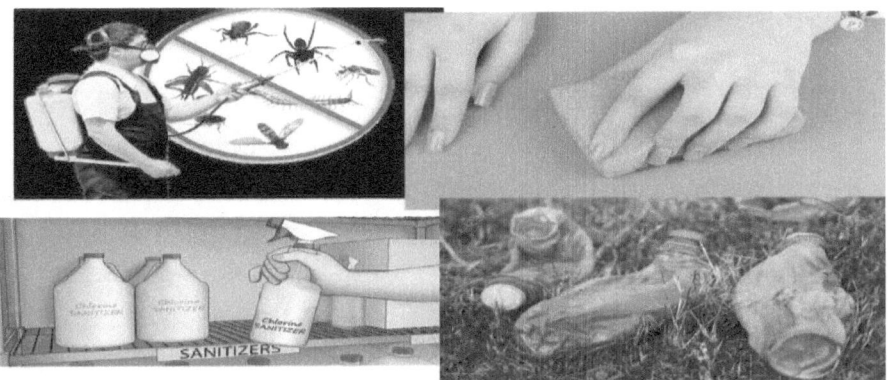

Utensils/Equipment containing potentially toxic metals

- Copper
- Brass
- Lead
- Zinc

Acidic and citric foods like tomatoes, oranges and lemons can react with these metals.

4.2.1. How can chemical contamination be prevented?

- Store chemicals away from food products. Label the chemicals for easy identification. Do not store any chemicals in a used food package/bottle.
- Do not reuse oil cans or bottles for storing other food ingredients. If you do that, there is a high chance of the product getting contaminated by oxidation. It can become rancid through the leftover strains of oil in the bottle.
- Ensure that all the chemical bottles are sealed and closed without any leakage.
- Ensure that the area is cleaned after pest-control has been carried out. This is essential to remove the chemical residues from the premises.
- Use chemicals according to the dilution level and recommended concentration specified in the label.
- Wash hands before and after handling chemicals.
- Do not use any plastics for the cooking or heating process, unless mentioned otherwise. Plastics, when used for heating, let out toxic elements that are hazardous to health. Use only those plastics that are suitable for microwave heating – food grade plastics like Polypropylene (No. 5) and High Density Polyethylene (No. 4).

4.3. Biological Contaminants/Hazards

As complicated as the term may sound, biological hazards are just microbial contaminants (bacteria, virus, fungi, parasites, biological toxins, etc.) that can cause severe food-borne illnesses.

Examples: seafood toxins, mushroom toxins, clostridium botulinum and salmonella.

4.3.1. How can biological contamination be prevented?

- Buy items only from vendors registered with and approved by FSSAI.
- Buy just what is needed. Do not over-stock. Over-stocking can lead to spoilage and wastage of your money.
- Discard mold-affected vegetables before the fungus/mold contaminates other vegetables also. Sort and grade properly at the store level to avoid such cases.
- Do not use any fish that has a slimy layer on its exterior.
- Ensure that you read the product label thoroughly before buying anything. This way, you can avoid buying food that is already spoilt.
- Maintain good personal hygiene and grooming standards. Wash hands as and when required - before and after handling raw, unprocessed or cooked food.
- Put in place a pest control system. Carry out pest control measures at least once a month, depending upon the nature of the food production involved.
- Control the humidity. Remember, more the moisture, higher the chances of microorganisms growing. Provide proper ventilation in the production areas to prevent suffocation of people, air-circulation and oil-draining.
- Control temperatures. Maintain cold food cold and hot food hot. If there are any leftovers, store them in the chiller and reheat them later. With respect to the premises, always ensure that the temperature is not beyond the 35°C-37°C range, which is the normal ambient temperature. Higher the temperature, more susceptible the food is to spoilage.
- Follow a cleaning schedule. Clean and sanitise facilities, machines and equipment frequently.
- Store dry foods, dry. Do not store them in a wet container.

4.4. Allergens

Allergens are substances that cause allergic reactions. These allergens are considered as the fourth type of hazards in the HACCP (Hazard Analysis Critical Control Point). Here are the major allergens in food:

1. Wheat/gluten

2. Eggs and egg products
3. Milk and milk products
4. Tree nuts- cashews, pistachios, hazelnuts, walnuts
5. Soya- soy products
6. Fish and fish products
7. Seafood, shrimp, prawns, lobsters, mussels, oysters, scallops
8. Crustaceans
9. Mushrooms

4.4.1. Handling allergens

Food Safety Allergen protocols to be followed in a food establishment.

- Awareness and training about the handling of all the allergens.
- Receiving and storing a dedicated area for easy identification and to prevent mishaps. These must be labeled appropriately.
- Use separate cooking vessels when handling and preparing "non-allergenic" food.
- Use of separate bins to keep the washed vessels. So that these do not get mixed up with other vessels.
- While serving, the servers must caution about the allergens added to the dish ordered. If not, mention in the menu under every meal.
- If, self-service, the menu display must contain a disclaimer stating about the allergens.
- For a packaged item, on the label, give a declaration stating the presence of allergens and traces of it.
- Even if it is a case of the equipment/ processing plant coming in contact with an allergen, the manufacture must declare stating traces of the allergen.

General Hygiene and Sanitary Practices

What are the minimum records and documents one must maintain?

- A laminated copy of your FSSAI Registration/License. This should be displayed at a prominent location in your premises.
- "Form C" and "Form E" (certificate of guarantee from your vendors and suppliers), and the bills issued by them on every visit.
- COA- Certificate of Analysis report from the supplier, once in every six months.
- The personal hygiene and grooming record of the staff members.
- Performa for medical fitness certificate for food handlers, issued by a registered medical practitioner and renewed once a year. This should cover physical examination, including that of the eyes and skin, and the enteric group of diseases like Tuberculosis and Typhoid. (yearly once)
- Maintaining a record of the following will be good:

  - Personal grooming record

- Kitchen temperature: cooking, serving and re-heating.
- Equipment/machine temperature.
- Daily, weekly, monthly, quarterly and half-yearly cleaning schedule and records, that will provide a complete traceability of issues. A sample checklist is being shared on the next page. Try to incorporate similar ones for other sections, too.
- The daily menu prepared in the kitchen, and bills issued to the customers.
- Customer complaints record.
- **Food test reports** - tested by an NABL lab. Basic microbiological parameters for coliforms and Total plate count to be done monthly. As per food safety guidelines, food testing is to be carried out at least once in 6 months for quality assurance (based on the product category and its testing parameters). It should also be done between batches for tracing batch-to-batch differences. Without food testing, the quality of food (which is most important to ensure the safety of consumers) cannot be assured.

- Compulsory swab test reports- monthly once for hands, chopping boards, knives, display or service plates, work surfaces, machinery and equipment.
- Water test reports- IS10500 - tested by an NABL lab (once a year).

EXAMPLE OF PERSONAL GROOMING RECORD

DATE:

S.No	Name of the staff	Body temperature Hair trimmed	PERSONAL GROOMING						PERSONAL HYGIENE	CHECKED BY	VERIFIED BY
			Beard shaved/ Mustache trimmed	Trimmed Nails	Ornaments/ Jewelry	Uniform (Aprons/ Shoes)	Head Cap	Religious threads	Hand wash		

GROOMING RECORD FOR KITCHEN/SERVICE STAFF

Grooming audit and checklist are generally followed to ensure proper personal hygiene of all the kitchen staff. Grooming audit is done every day, and is recorded in the format given earlier. Clean, fresh uniforms, head gear, cut nails, clean-shaven face, closed footwear and trim hair are good standards of grooming. No band/thread/watch or jewellery is to be worn by the production staff.

EXAMPLE OF PERFORMA FOR STAFF MEDICAL FITNESS

PERFORMA FOR MEDICAL FITNESS CERTIFICATE FOR FOOD HANDLERS

(FOR THE YEAR ....)

(See Para No. 10.1.2, Part- II, Schedule - 4 of FSS Regulation, 2011)

It is certified that Shri/Smt./Miss...

employed with M/s.., coming in direct contact with food items has been carefully examined* by me on date ....

Based on the medical examination conducted, he/she is found free from any infectious or communicable diseases and the person is fit to work in the above mentioned food establishment.

Name and Signature with Seal
of Registered Medical Practitioner /
Civil Surgeon

*Medical Examination to be conducted:

1. Physical Examination
2. Eye Test
3. Skin Examination
4. Compliance with schedule of Vaccine to be inoculated against enteric group of diseases
5. Any test required to confirm any communicable or infectious disease which the person suspected to be suffering from on clinical examination.

EXAMPLE OF MASTER CLEANING SCHEDULE/RECORD/CHECKLIST

SECTION/AREA: Production or Kitchen

AREAS/EQUIPMENT TO BE CLEANED	FREQUENCY/ PER WEEK	MON	TUE	WED	THURS	FRI	SAT	SUN	PERSON WHO CLEANED
KITCHEN COUNTERS	7								
SHELVES	4								
FLOOR (HARD REACH)	4								
FLOOR (GENERAL, EVERYDAY AFTER SHIFT)	7								
WALLS	4								
CEILING	2								
TABLES	2- AFTER USE								
LIGHTS	2								
FOOD EQUIPMENT	AFTER USE								
EXHAUST FANS	1								
CHIMNEY	1								

Checked by:

Verified by:

Remarks, if any:

How frequently should I test my products?

You must test raw and processed food (hot and cold) once a month to check if it is fit for consumption (basic microbiological parameters for coliforms and total plate count). Meanwhile, FSSAI has issued a guideline stating that the finished product shall be tested for microbiological parameters as per FSS (Food Safety Standards)at least once in 6 months, depending on the food group it falls in (check the FSSAI food catergorisation code). Similarly, the potability of water must be tested once in 6 months as per IS10500- chemically and + Cooking oil to be tested for TPC (Total Polar Compounds) and Peroxide value once every 6 months.

List of microbial/ chemical/ physio-chemical tests for catering sector (to be tested once in 6 months)

S No	Food Group	Microbiological Parameters	Physio-chemical Parameters
1	All food products (except below and swab samples, food contact materials)	Total Plate Count (TPC), Ecoli, Coliform count, Staphylococcus - spp, Salmonella. spp,	
2	Raw veg and cooked veg	E Coli, Listeria. spp	
3	Meat and meat products	Straphylococcus aureus, Salmonella. spp, Listeria Monocytogenes, Aerobic plate count, Yeast and Mold, Sulphite reducing Clostridia, Clostridium Botulinum, (Canded/retort), Campylobacter. spp (canded/retort)	Moisture, protein, fat
4	Poultry	Straphylococcus aureus, Salmonella. spp, Aerobic plate count, Yeast and Mold, E Coli, Sulphite reducing Clostridia, Clostridium Botulinum, (Canded/retort), Enterobacter sakazakii (Cronobacter. Spp)	Moisture, protein, fat
5	Bakery Products	Yeast and Mold, Salmonella, Listeria, Staphylococcus aureus, E Coli	pH, Bulk density, moisture, total ash. Low volume (bread), specific volume (bread), thickness (cookies), diameter (cookies), spread ratio (cookies)
6	Water and Ice	As per FSSAI requirements - IS 10500	As per FSSAI requirements and colour, odour, taste, turbidity, pH, TDS (total dissolved solids), TH (total hardness), iron content, chloride content, nitrate content.
7	Sea food	TPC, Ecoli, Vibriocholarae, Vibrioparahaemolyticus, Staphylococcus aureus, Shigella. spp, Salmonella. spp, Listeria monocytogens	Acidity (pH), moisture, protein, fat, histamine content, TVBN (Total Volatile Base Nitrogen)
8	Milk and Milk products	TPC, Ecoli, Coliforms, Listeria Monocytogenes, Staphylococcus aureus, Bascillus cereus, Sulphate reducing clostridia, Salmonella. spp, Yeast and Mold	Titratable acidity (pH), nitrogen content, total casein (protein), lactose content, specific gravity, fat and SNF.

Cleaning and Sanitisation

What is the difference between cleaning and sanitation?

Cleaning removes all visible dirt, soil, chemical residue and allergens from the equipment, utensils and work surfaces.

Sanitation reduces the number of micro-organisms to a safe level. **Sanitisation is performed after cleaning**. Unclean surfaces will reduce the effectiveness of sanitising. All surfaces that come into contact with food must be cleaned and then sanitised regularly.

Sanitising should not be confused with sterilizing. While sanitising reduces micro-organisms to a safe level, sterilizing removes all micro-organisms from an item. It mostly involves blanching, steaming and pressure cooking.

What do I have to clean and sanitise?

As a general rule, everything that has had direct contact with food needs to be cleaned and sanitised daily.

Examples of items that may have had direct contact with food include crockery, glassware, cutlery, pots and pans, serving utensils, cooking equipment, chopping boards, kitchen surfaces and counters.

Other items – that have not had direct contact with food – must be cleaned, but need not be sanitised. Such items include chairs, tables, floors, doors, floors, walls and windows. Don't forget to clean areas that are hard to reach, such as under cushions, around light fittings, blinds and drapes. Clean the drains and restrooms at least once a day.

The cleaning schedule should include instructions for when and how to clean floors, sinks, walls, counters, chairs, tables, etc.

How do I clean and sanitise fruits and vegetables?

Fruits and vegetables can be sanitised with diluted chlorine (4ml in 10 litres of water).

Since we are talking about a small-scale restaurant, you can use lukewarm salt water or a diluted vinegar solution to clean and sanitise fruits and vegetables.

You must clean and sanitise the vegetables used raw in salads and sandwiches – such as lettuce, cabbage, tomatoes and green leafy vegetables -with salt water before dressing them.

The following fruits and vegetables are to be soaked in saltwater, and rinsed thoroughly with cold water: strawberries, spinach, kale, apples, grapes, peaches, cherries, pears, tomatoes, celery, potatoes and hot peppers.

This is how you should wash vegetables and fruits with the soaking method:

- Sanitise the sink: wash hands, and use soap and water to clean all the areas of the sink that will come into contact with your fresh produce.
- Fill the sink with lukewarm water, diluted salt water or vinegar solution. Use a 1:30 ratio of wash to water.
- Soak vegetables for at least 3 minutes in the sink.

- Place them in a colander/big vessel-filter, and use hands to rub the produce while rinsing with cold water.
- Let them air-dry.

Spray Method

Vegetables with firmer skin, such as eggplant, potatoes, yam and cucumbers, may benefit from a spray and scrub. This will thoroughly clean dirt and pesticides from their surface. This method is also ideal for larger, smooth fruits and vegetables that don't have crevices or cracks.

For effective cleaning of your fruits and vegetables, follow these steps:

- Wash hands and all areas coming into contact with your fresh produce with soap and water.
- Fill a spray bottle with diluted vinegar solution, and spray the entire surface of each vegetable or fruit.
- Let the coated produce sit for at least 30 seconds.
- Use your hands or a vegetable cleaning brush to scrub the produce, and rinse the solution off in cold running water. Ensure that the brush bristles used for scrubbing are not loose, and are used only for this purpose.
- Let the fruits and vegetables air-dry.

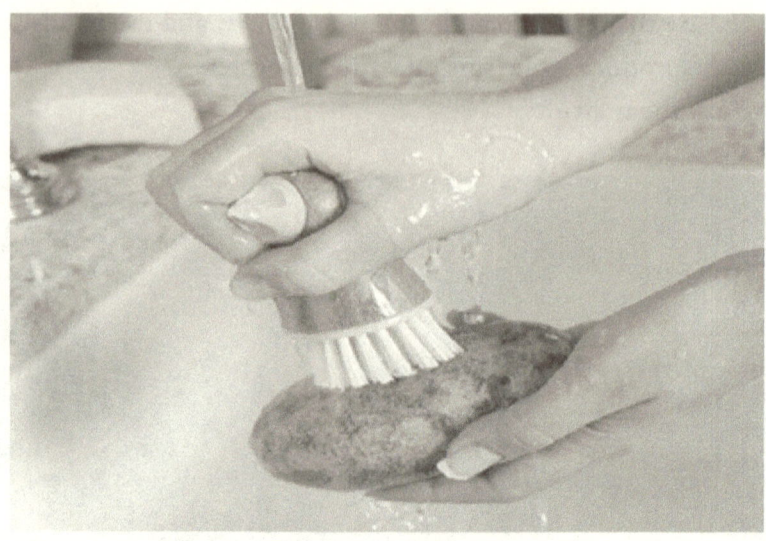

How do I clean, wash and sanitise eggs that have a lot of dirt?

While receiving eggs, ensure that you sort and grade the good ones. Do not accept eggs that have a lot of bird droppings. Some eggs come with dirt, soil and sticky bits. You can clean these with hot water, and scrub-clean them. You can dip the eggs in 50 PPM (4 ml in 10 litres of water) chlorine solution. Scrub-clean them, and let them air-dry thoroughly.

How do I sanitise the kitchen counter and the workspace?

You can follow the previously-mentioned "spray and dry with a clean towel" method, once after every batch. The easier way to sanitise your counters is by using a 70% alcohol solution.

How frequently do I have to clean my equipment and containers?

Have a proper schedule for cleaning equipment and machines. It's always good to clean them at the end of the day. Ensure that you clean the common-touch points frequently. After cleaning, always dry them thoroughly.

How do I wash and sanitise my chopping boards and knives?

Chopping boards harbour a lot of micro-organisms. It is always recommended that you have separate chopping boards for veg and non-veg products. Chopping boards are to be cleaned, sanitised and dried after every use.

Chopping boards can be sanitised by:

- Using a diluted solution of vinegar and baking powder.
- Using a chlorine solution. Use 50 PPM (4 ml in 10 litres of water) for veg chopping boards and 100 PPM (8ml in 10 litres of water) for non-veg chopping boards.
- Using chlorine tablets. 50 PPM (2 tablets in 30 litres of water) for veg. and 100 PPM (4 tablets in 30 litres of water) for non-veg.
- Using a 1% sodium hypochlorite solution.
- Immersing it in 90°C hot water after every use.
- Immersing it in a solution of lukewarm lime water.

Immerse the boards in one of these diluted solutions for at least 3 hours for them to react with the board. Then, rinse the boards with warm water and leave them to dry.

Knives are to be sanitised after every use or at the end of the day by dipping them in hot water and drying them properly. They can be sanitised with diluted vinegar or diluted chlorine of 50 PPM (4ml in 10 litres of water) also. After that, rinse them with warm water.

If you think it is dangerous to use many chemicals to sanitise these boards and knives, here are a few alternative ways.

Cleaning and sanitising of chopping boards and knives without chemicals

1. Prepare and Clean	• Sanitise the sink. Wash hands before handling. • Remove dirt, loose items and any other physical contaminants.
2. Wash and Sanitise	• Sanitise with hot water (60°C) for at least 2-3 minutes. • You can also sanitise with diluted vinegar (1:30).
3. Rinse and Air-Dry	• Rub and rinse with clean lukewarm potable water and a clean cloth. • Leave them to air-dry.

Cleaning and Sanitisation of chopping boards and knives with chemicals

1. Preparation and Cleaning	• Sanitise the sink. Wash hands before handling • Remove dirt, loose items or any other physical contaminants.
2a. Wash and Sanitise for Liquid Chlorine	• Sanitise with 50 PPM liquid chlorine:4 ml in 10L for vegetables and fruits ; 8ml in 10L for non-veg chopping boards (100PPM).
2b. Wash and Sanitise for Chlorine Tablets	• For veg chopping boards- use 2 tablets in 30L (50PPM) of water and for non-veg chopping boards- 4 tablets in 30L of water (100PPM).
3. Rinse and Dry	•Dip in the diluted chlorine for about 3 hours for it to react with the product immersed. Rinse them with warm water. •Leave them to dry.

How do I clean and sanitise machine and equipment that have oil stains and grease?

The mesh:

If the exhaust fans have mesh filters, remove them and pour boiling water through them. Soak them in a mixture of hot water and ammonia (1/2 cup ammonia per gallon of water) for an hour. Remove the mesh from the soaking solution, and scrub the solution around the mesh. It's not just the filter that accumulates fat; even the fan blades do that. Wear a mask when you use this ammonia solution.

The fan blades:

Prepare a mix of water and soap. Alternatively, you can add a mixture of 2tbsp 1/4 ammonia and 2tbsp baking soda to a full cup of warm water. Put on the rubber gloves and, using the above mixture and cotton cloth, scrub the exhaust fan blades. Then scrub the rest of the fan's body.

Breaking down grease:

Caustic chemicals can be applied to break down grease. After that, hot water can be used to rinse away the residue.

Control of Operations/Process

Is it necessary for me to use a thermometer and check the temperature of the food I prepare?

Yes, it's always better to do a temperature check on every dish prepared. This will make it easier to track the root cause of any food spoilage later on, and deal with customer complaints. Traceability is one of the ways by which the root cause can be analysed: by tracking all along the process chain and identifying the fault.

Is it okay to reheat food in a microwave over?

Yes, it is. But it is not advisable to reheat more than once. Microwave ovens emit rays which are harmful to the food.

Why should we not reheat food more than twice, even through other methods of heating?

Danger Zone Temperature (DZT) is the temperature range where there is a higher chance of microbial growth which leads to food-borne illnesses. The image below explains the stages of microbial growth and destruction.

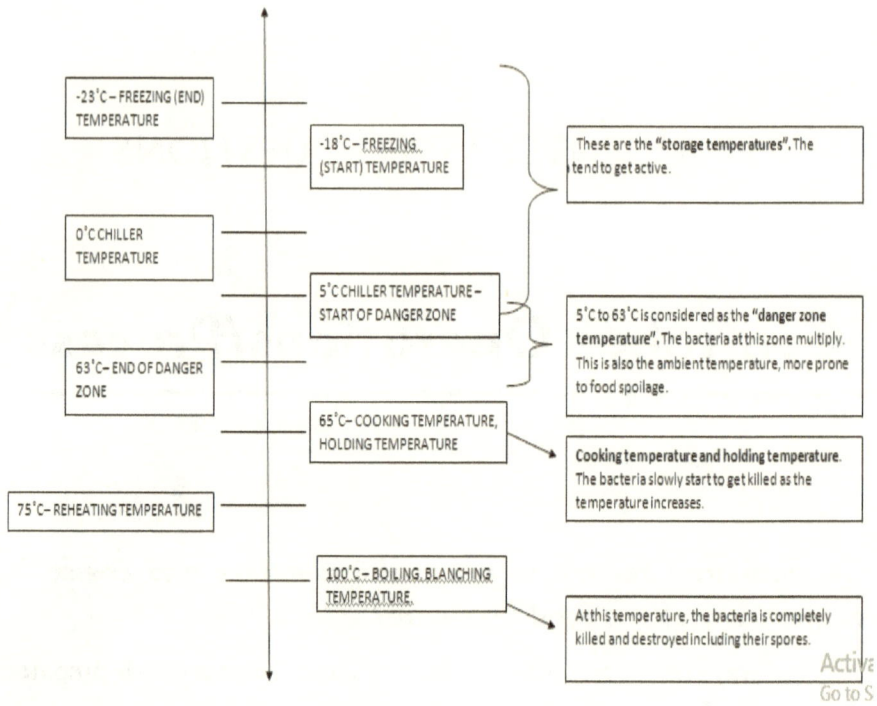

For instance, if you have leftover gravy, you store them in the chiller. When needed, you heat them and store them in the chiller again. If you notice, there's a fluctuation of temperatures from higher to lower to higher to – again - lower. Micro-organisms tend to thrive in ambient temperature **(5°C to 65°C - danger zone temperature)**, especially on foods that have more water content and moisture. This is why dry products have a longer shelf-life; they have no water content.

Repeated re-heating of food product leads to a major temperature fluctuation, leaving the product unpalatable and unhealthy. It is not recommended for consumption. By repeated reheating, the product is more susceptible to spoilage. Also, there is a higher risk of food poisoning, if that food is consumed.

What are the methods of thawing a frozen product?

Chiller thawing

- Take the required content from the freezer, and store it in the chiller overnight (at least for 8-12 hours).
- Cover the container while thawing in the chiller.
- Keep the product that is thawing on the lower rack, so that there is no dripping loss or contamination of other products stored in the chiller.
- Only after the product has completely melted/softened, should you use it for cooking.

Chiller thawing on the lower rack

Cold water thawing

- Keep the contents dipped in a sink of cold running water for at least 90 minutes. Yes, that's a long time, and a lot of water will be consumed in this process. But, you can find ways to reuse this water. For instance, you can redirect it to the garden, or find a way to connect it to softener water tanks through an outlet pipe.

- Every half an hour, change the position of the dipped food contents for thorough thawing.
- Do not dip the contents in still water. In that case, there is a higher chance of foul smell and breeding taking place.
- Take this to the next step only when the whole product is evenly thawed.

Cold water thawing

What is RUCO?

Re-purposed Used Cooking Oil is an initiative by FSSAI to enable conversion of used cooking oil to biodiesel, so that the diversion of used cooking oil back into the food chain is reduced.

How can FBOs dispose of their used cooking oil?

Checkhttps://fssai. gov. in/ruco/, where the list of biodiesel aggregators is given.

Is it necessary to segregate waste?

Yes. Not segregating waste leads to higher pest infestation, foul smell and other toxic residues.

- The waste/garbage bins must be sturdy and non-leaking, and should have a disposable cover.
- Cleaning and sanitising the bins regularly must be a part of the cleaning schedule.
- Discard the wet waste away from the kitchen. Dry waste can be kept in a bin in the kitchen, but away from the food counter.
- Do not leave the cover of the waste bin open, or have the bin overflowing, because that would attract more flies and aid their breeding.
- Discard the waste at proper time intervals (as soon as the bin is about 3/4thfull). And after you do so, please wash your hands with a soap solution.

What are the efficient ways to cool food?

Food needs aid to cool down quickly. The below factors affects the process of cooling:-

- **Size of the food:** The thicker the food, longer time it takes to cool down.
- **Density of the food:** Denser the food, longer time it takes to cool down.
- **Container in which the food is stored:** Stainless steel heats the food faster when compared to other types of containers.
- **Size of the container:** Shallow containers/ pans allow the heat from the food to disperse faster than the deeper ones.

The efficient ways to cool food include:

- Ice water-bath and frequent stirring of the food for rapid cooling.
- Adding ice as in ingredient in case of liquid food.
- Storing ladles/ spoons in a cold water or frozen water. To use that for stirring for rapid cooling.

Service, Distribution and Transportation

How often do I have to replace the water in the bain-marie?

Change every batch after every meal-breakfast, lunch, snack, dinner. If possible, change it every two hours. The water has to be maintained at a standard 65°C temperature throughout the batch.

What is the right hot and cold holding temperature?

The temperature of a buffet counter or any other hot holding counter must be 65°C or above. For cold holding counters, it must be between 0°C and 5°C.

What hygiene standards must one follow for a take-out option?

The rule is the same. Ensure that all the staff involved in serving the take-out, adhere to the personal hygiene and grooming standards mentioned earlier in this book. Also, they must wear PPE (Personal Protective Equipment) like head gear, gloves, aprons and masks.

Sanitise the take-out or pick-up area as and when needed. Ensure cashless transactions. Sanitise the food containers before putting the food in. Ensure that you provide only QR-coded menu cards to avoid transmission of viruses.

Packaging and Labelling

I'm selling a single-ingredient product. Do I need to have detailed labelling?

You don't need details like nutritional information and ingredients on the label, as it has just a single ingredient. The other details, like the name of the product, net weight in grams, customer care information, allergen information (if any), manufacturing address, batch number, date of preparation and the "best before date" are to be mentioned.

Do I have to label my product if the shelf life is only 24-48 hours?

It is not mandatory. But you must give clear information about

- instructions for usage and storage
- date and time of preparation
- use-by date of the product.
- allergen details (if any)
- the veg/non-veg declaration
- customer care details.

If the product is to last beyond 3 days and on retail shelves, it is necessary to follow the mandatory labelling requirements put forth by FSSAI.

You can visit www. fssai. gov. in to read their new guidelines on packaging and labelling.

What type of food-grade plastic can I use for service and delivery purposes?

Use PP No. 5 or HDPE No. 2 of food grade plastics. You can look at the numbers given under every plastic container or bottle. Ensure that you don't store hot food in a plastic container and seal it immediately. If you do that, there is a higher chance of the plastic melting and the chemical leaching. In the case of beverages, smoothies or milkshakes, the recommended plastic type is PET No. 1. But these bottles/containers are not reusable. They must be crushed and discarded after a single-use. With a ban being imposed on single-use plastics, it is advisable to use eco-friendly bio-degradable containers. Some of the popular bio-degradable containers available in the markets are:

- Wheat straw hinged clamshell containers

- Compostable hinged Sugarcane takeout containers or Sugarcane Clamshells

- Bio-plastics made out of plants.
- Replace plastics with Papers.
- Plant based or beverage cups.

What are the Food Grade Plastics?

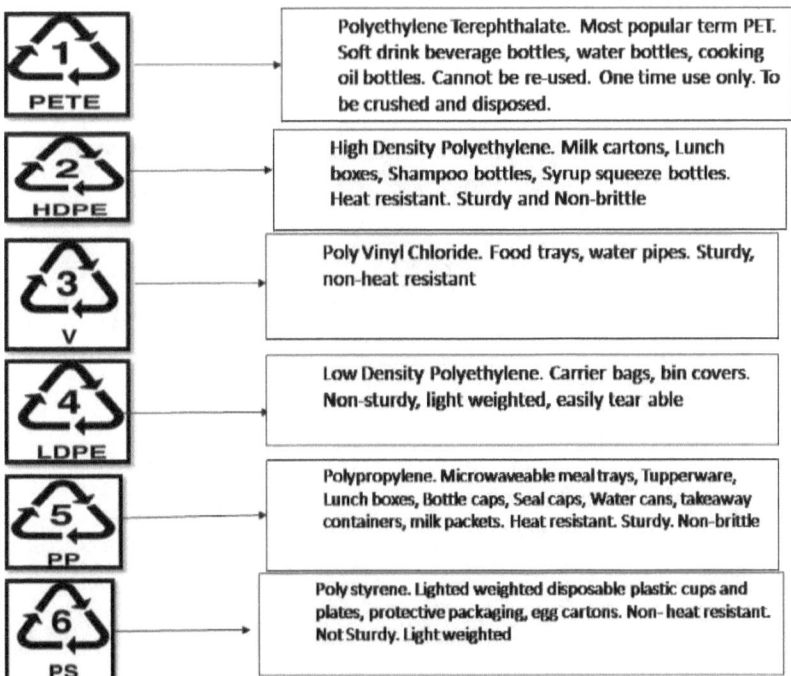

PETE (1)	Polyethylene Terephthalate. Most popular term PET. Soft drink beverage bottles, water bottles, cooking oil bottles. Cannot be re-used. One time use only. To be crushed and disposed.
HDPE (2)	High Density Polyethylene. Milk cartons, Lunch boxes, Shampoo bottles, Syrup squeeze bottles. Heat resistant. Sturdy and Non-brittle
V (3)	Poly Vinyl Chloride. Food trays, water pipes. Sturdy, non-heat resistant
LDPE (4)	Low Density Polyethylene. Carrier bags, bin covers. Non-sturdy, light weighted, easily tear able
PP (5)	Polypropylene. Microwaveable meal trays, Tupperware, Lunch boxes, Bottle caps, Seal caps, Water cans, takeaway containers, milk packets. Heat resistant. Sturdy. Non-brittle
PS (6)	Poly styrene. Lighted weighted disposable plastic cups and plates, protective packaging, egg cartons. Non- heat resistant. Not Sturdy. Light weighted

Food Grade Plastics (FGP) is those plastics that are safe to pack food and drinks. They should not leach chemicals (BPA) upon cooking and storage, which is chemically hazardous to health and other aspects. The numbers mentioned above in a triangle symbol are all the main types of plastics available. Of these, the below picture will show the Food Grade plastics.

FGP's can be identified by the "wine glass and fork" symbol, which indicates that the particular plastic is safe for cooking and storage of food and drinks. A more natural way to identify the type of plastic is to locate these signs underneath your plastic and identify the brand. For example:-

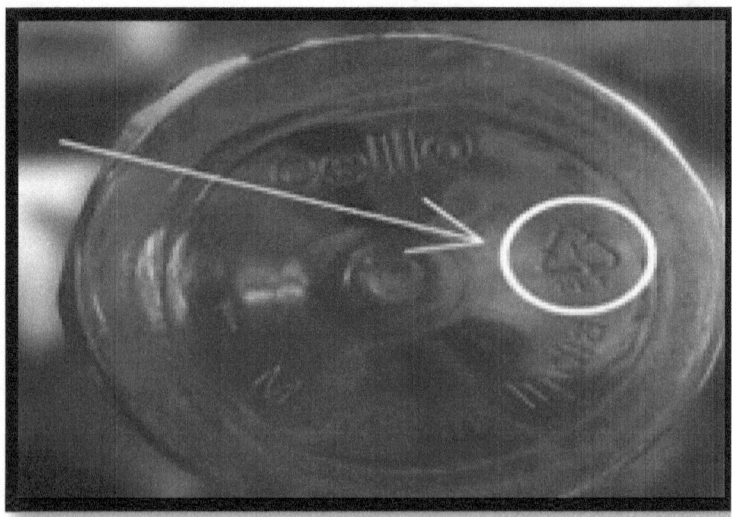

What are the mandatory labelling requirements?

1. Name of the Brand/ company
2. Name of the Product
3. Veg/non-veg declaration
4. Net weight in grams (g)
5. List of Ingredients (descending order)
6. Declaration of food additives
7. Nutritional information (Energy, protein, carbohydrate, Total sugars, Trans fat, Fat)
8. Allergen declaration
9. Storage instructions and Instructions for usage
10. FSSAI License
11. Manufacturer address
12. Date of Manufacturing/production/ packaging
13. Use by date/ Best before date
14. Lot no/ code no/ batch no
15. Maximum retail price
16. Customer care no and details

Pest Control

How often do I need to carry out pest control in my kitchen?

- Find a pest control agency that is registered and certified to carry out pest control.
- You can visit my website www. pavithrakrishnaprasad. com and read the articles about pest control, along with the details of agencies that are good at it.
- Pest control for a kitchen will depend upon the activity and the space. Usually, it is good to do it once in 15 days.
- It is better to not use electric rackets to kill flies. Using them increases the chance of the flies falling into the food and the floor.

What are the major pests, insects and rodents I must watch out for?

Insects: German cockroaches, flies.
Pests: Moths, beetles, weevils, mites.
Rodents: Rats, mice.
Birds: Pigeons, doves.

All these carry and spread harmful bacteria. Prevent them from getting into any food storage or handling area.

What are the home-based pest control measures I can take?

- Use meshes on windows.
- Check inward and outward packages for infestation by small pests and insects. You can check if the packages have rat-bite marks or small holes. Also check if the seal is open or the cans are puffed/bloated.
- Do not use cardboard boxes, cartons, newspapers or any wooden materials that attract pests.
- Keep garbage bins covered always.
- Get a professional agency to carry out pest control once a month or every 15 days, depending on the nature of the production.
- Never spray any chemicals during the production or service of food. There is a higher chance of chemical contamination, if you do so.
- Do not use electric rackets to kill mosquitoes or flies. There is a higher chance of these dead flies or insects falling into the production premises. Hence, Pest Electric Devices/insectocutors are used instead of the rackets to capture and trap small pests and flies. These devices are to be placed 5 feet above the ground, and opposite to the flow of air and opposite to the entrance.
- Using rat traps should be avoided, as that could lead to having a dead rat rotting within the premises. Rat cakes should also be avoided, because rats could consume the cake and then contaminate the food products. That will be poisonous, and can even be fatal.
- Ensure that there are no rodent droppings.
- All drainages to be covered with a grill and a mesh. Cockroach traps and pre-filters to be placed properly in the drainage.
- Store only what is needed, and do not over-stock. Over-stocking leads to higher chances of weevils and beetles infesting the old, dry products.

Cross-Contamination

What are the types of cross-contamination?

Contamination is classified into three major types:

Food-to-food contamination
Examples:

- Handling veg and non-veg products together. It is recommended that you have separate chopping boards for veg and non-veg products.
- Storing non-veg and veg items together.
- Storing raw materials with cooked food. This can contaminate the raw food.

Image courtesy: Wiki How. com

Hand-to-food contamination
Examples:

- Touching cooked food with bare hands while serving.
- Touching contaminated food, or touching food with dirty hands/fingers. The image below shows a street food vendor handling food/ ingredients with bare hands.

Equipment-to-food contamination
Examples:

- Using toxic metals for cooking. Handling rusted equipment.
- Using unclean, un-sanitised equipment.
- When one of the parts of the equipment becomes loose, and falls into the food.
- Cooking with non-food-grade materials.

Training and Awareness

Is there any training/awareness or certification program that I must undergo?

- Yes. For every 25 members from a food establishment, one person must undergo FOSTAC- Food Safety Supervisor for Basic Catering/ Manufacturing.
- FOSTAC is a food safety training and certification program put forward by FSSAI.
- A certificate will be given to you, along with a number that is valid for one year from the date of issue. After that, it should be renewed.
- You can visit www. fostac. fssai. gov. in for details about upcoming training sessions.
- This training & certification program is specifically for street food vendors, primary manufacturers, home-based caterers, hawkers, storage and transport agencies (with less than 100 vehicles) and small retailers.

I want my staff members to understand basic hygiene standards. Who should I approach?

You can e-mail me your requirements. I will be happy to give your staff the necessary basic training.

The training will be held once or twice a month, depending on the nature of the production, and the size of the staff involved. It will focus on creating awareness of basic food safety practices among the handlers and staff involved in the food production. Some of the aspects that will be covered are:

- Correct ways to store and handle fresh produce and packed food.
- Personal hygiene and grooming.
- Cleaning, sanitation and drying.
- Food spoilage and food-borne illnesses
- Cross contamination
- Different food temperatures
- Food hazards

Please write to me at fsg@pavithrakrishnaprasad. com, or reach me through my website www. pavithrakrishnaprasad. com

What is a Food Safety Display Board?

As per FSSAI, it is mandatory for FBOs to display the FSSAI Registration/License and certificate at their premises. Usually, the FSSAI license number is not visible to consumers. And so, to instil confidence in them, and to strengthen food safety, FSSAI has introduced the Food Safety Display Board (FSDB). FBOs have to display the FSDBs at their premises.

FSDBs are informative boards that display the food safety and hygiene practices being followed by the FBO in their establishment.

FSDBs are colour-coded for different kinds of food businesses, for ease of recognition.

- An FSDB displays the FSSAI registration/license number of the FBO, which the customer can verify on the FSSAI website.
- It informs the customers about the 12 golden rules (refer the following image), thus giving them full assurance and confidence on food safety.
- It displays an effective consumer feedback system, providing various options to consumers for sending feedback to FSSAI: including WhatsApp, SMS and the FSSAI App (Food Safety Connect).

If you run a pick-up or takeaway service, it is mandatory for you to display this board in that area, so that it is visible to the customers. Enter your registration number, company name and GST details in your FSDB.

Size of the FSDB: A4 size for FSSAI Registered food business; A3 for FSSAI Licensed food business.

Material of the FSDB: The material must be such that the contents of the board don't get blurred or damaged over time.

Directions for FBOs: You can add your FSSAI registration/license number at the top of the board, and the name of the company and feedback-related details in the lower part.

FOOD SAFETY DISPLAY BOARD

License No. (Please Mention Your License no.) ■ Restaurant

With Us You Will Get Safe Food
We Follow These 12 Golden Rules

Hygiene Rule Codes		Hygiene Rule Codes	
1	Keep premise clean and have regular pest control	Wear clean clothes/ uniform	**7**
2	Use potable water for food preparation	Wash hands before & after handling food and after using toilets, coughing, sneezing, etc.	**8**
3	Cook food thoroughly. Keep hot food above 60°C and cold food below 5°C	Use water proof bandage to cover cuts or burn wounds	**9**
4	Store veg & non veg food, raw & cooked food in separate containers	Do not handle food when unwell	**10**
5	Store cold food below 5°C and frozen products at -18°C or below	Use clean and separate dusters to clean surfaces and wipe utensils	**11**
6	Use separate chopping boards, knives, etc. for raw/ cooked & veg/non veg food	Keep separate & covered dustbins for food waste	**12**

If any concern

Give your Feedback to Company Name

🕿 Call toll free
1800 112 100

◎ SMS or Whatsapp
9868686868
Always quote FSSAI Number for quick action

(Company Name)
(Contact Details) 🕿
◎

Download FSSAI APP
or Logon to https://foodlicensing.fssai.gov.in/cmsweb

Connect with us:
ⓕ Food Safety and Standards Authority of India
ⓣ fssaiindia

Glossary

COA- Certificate of Analysis
COG- Certificate of Guarantee
DZT: Danger Zone Temperature
FBO: Food Business Operators
FIFO: First In First Out
FEFO: First Expiry First Out
FSSAI: Food Safety Standards Authority of India
Form A: Application for Registration/renewal of Registration under the FSS Act-2006
Form B: Application for License/renewal of License under FSS Act-2006
Form C: License format
FoSCoS: Food Safety Compliance System
FLRS: Food Licensing Registration System
FSDB: Food Safety Display Board
KOB: Kind of Business
MT: Metric tonne
NOC: No Objection Certificate

PPE: Personal Protective Equipment
PPM: Parts per million
UCO: Used Cooking Oil
RUCO: Repurposed Used Cooking Oil
TPC: Total Plate Count
TH: Total Hardness
TDS: Total Dissolved Solids

Annexure

Hygiene rating checklist for an establishment to be certified as "safe place to eat"

Mandatory Requirements for Catering (Hygiene Rating)

FSSAI Supervisor Name:

Name of the Establishment:

FSS Certificate No.:

FSSAI Registration Number:

Rows where S.No is marked with asterisks are mandatory questions.

Similarly, questions with an asterisk (*)may significantly impact food safety and therefore, must be addressed on priority basis. Failure in any of these questions will mean non-compliance.

You can score a maximum total of 114.

S. NO	AUDIT QUESTION	SCORING	
		MAX. POSSIBLE SCORE	SCORE OBTAINED
1	The food establishment has an updated FSSAI license, and that is displayed at a prominent location.	2	
Design & facilities			
2	The design of the food premises provides adequate working space; permits maintenance & cleaning to prevent the entry of dirt, dust & pests.	2	
3	The internal structure & fittings are made of non-toxic and impermeable material.	2	
4	Walls, ceilings & doors are free from flaking paint or plaster, condensation& shedding particles.	2	
5	Floors are non-absorbent, non-slippery & sloped appropriately.	2	
6	Windows are kept closed &are fitted with insect-proof screen when opening to external environment.	2	
7	Doors are smooth & non-absorbent. Suitable precautions have been taken to prevent entry of pests.	2	
8*	Potable water (meeting standards of IS:10500& tested semi-annually, with records maintained thereof) is used as product ingredient, or is in contact with food or food contact surface.	2	
9	Equipment and containers are made of non-toxic, impervious, non-corrosive material, which is easy to clean & disinfect.	2	
10	There are adequate facilities for heating, cooling, refrigeration and freezing food&to facilitate monitoring of temperature.	2	
11*	Premiseshas sufficient lighting. Lighting fixtures are protected to prevent contamination on breakage.	2	

S. NO	AUDIT QUESTION	SCORING	
		MAX. POSSIBLE SCORE	SCORE OBTAINED
12	Adequate ventilation is provided within the premises.	2	
13	Adequate storage facilities for food, packaging materials, chemicals, personal items, etc. are available.	2	
14	Personnel hygiene facilities are available, including an adequate number of hand washing facilities, toilets and change rooms for employees.	2	
15*	Food material is tested, either through an internal laboratory or through an accredited lab. Check for records.	2	
Control of operations			
16*	Incoming material is procured as per internally laid-down specification from approved vendors. Check for records (like certificate of analysis, Form E, specifications, name and address of the supplier, batch no., mfg., use by/expiry date, quantity procured, etc.)	2	
17	Raw materials are inspected at the time of receiving for food safety hazards. (Farm produce like vegetables, fruits, eggs, etc. must be checked for spoilage & accepted only in good condition.)	2	
18	Incoming material, semi or final products are stored according to their temperature requirement in a hygienic environment to avoid deterioration and to protect them from contamination. (Foods of animal origin are stored at a temperature less than or equal to 4°C.)	2	
19	All raw materials are cleaned thoroughly before food preparation.	2	
20*	Proper segregation of raw and cooked vegetarian and non-vegetarian food is done.	2	

S. NO	AUDIT QUESTION	SCORING	
		MAX. POSSIBLE SCORE	SCORE OBTAINED
21	All the equipment is adequately sanitised before and after food preparation.	2	
22*	Frozen food is thawed hygienically. No thawed food is stored for later use. (Meat, fish and poultry are thawed in the refrigerator between 0°C and 5°C or in a microwave oven. Shellfish/seafood is thawed in cold potable running water at 15°C or less, within 90 minutes of thawing.	2	
23*	Vegetarian items are cooked to a minimum of 60°C for 10 minutes or 65°C for 2 minutes core food temperature. Non- vegetarian items are cooked for a minimum of 65°C for 10 minutes or 70°C for 2 minutes or 75°C for 15 seconds core food temperature.	2	
24*	Cooked food intended for refrigeration is cooled appropriately. (High-risk food is cooled from 60°C to 21°C within 2 hours or less & further cooled to 5°C within two hours or less.)	2	
25*	Food portioning is done under hygienic conditions. High- risk food is portioned in a refrigerated area or portioned and refrigerated within 30 minutes. Large amount of food is portioned below 15°C.	2	
26*	Hot veg-food intended for consumption is held at 65°C and hot non-vegetarian food intended for consumption is held at 70°C. Cold foods are maintained at 5°C or below, and frozen products are held at -18°C or below.	2	
27*	Reheating is done appropriately, and no indirect reheating such as adding hot water or reheating under bainmaire or reheating under lamp is being used. (The core temperature of food reaches 75°C and is reheated for at least 2 minutes at this temperature.)	2	

S. NO	AUDIT QUESTION	SCORING	
		MAX. POSSIBLE SCORE	SCORE OBTAINED
28	Oil suitable for cooking purposes is being used. Periodic verification of fat and oil by checking the colour, flavour and floated elements is being done.	2	
29*	Vehicles intended for food transportation are kept clean and maintained in good repair, and are maintain at the required temperature. (Hot foods are kept at 65°C, cold foods at 5°C and frozen items at -18°C during transportation within 2 hours of food preparation.)	2	
30	Food and non-food products transported at same time in the same vehicle are separated adequately to avoid any risk to food.	2	
31	Cutlery, crockery used for serving and dinner accompaniments at dining service are clean, and sanitised free form unhygienic matter.	2	
32*	Packaging and wrapping material coming in contact with food is clean and of food grade quality.	2	
Maintenance & sanitation			
33*	Cleaning of equipment, food premises is done as per cleaning schedule & cleaning program. There should be no stagnation of water in food zones.	2	
34	Preventive maintenance of equipment and machinery is carried out regularly as per the instructions of the manufacturer. Check for records.	2	
35	Measuring & monitoring devices are calibrated periodically.	2	
36	Pest control program is available, and pest control activities are carried out by trained and experienced personnel. Check for records.	2	
37*	No signs of pest activity or infestation in premises (eggs, larvae, faeces, etc.)	2	

S. NO	AUDIT QUESTION	SCORING	
		MAX. POSSIBLE SCORE	SCORE OBTAINED
38	Drains are designed to meet expected flow loads, and are equipped with grease and cockroach traps to capture contaminants and pests.	2	
39	Food waste and other refuse are removed periodically from food-handling areas to avoid accumulation.	2	
Personal hygiene			
40*	Annual medical examination & inoculation of food handlers against the enteric group of diseases as per recommended schedule of the vaccine is done. Check for records.	2	
41*	No person suffering from a disease or illness or with open wounds or burns is involved in handling of food or materials which come in contact with food.	2	
42*	Food handlers maintain personal cleanliness (clean clothes, trimmed nails, water-proof bandage, etc.) and correct personal behaviour (hand washing, no loose jewellery, no smoking, no spitting, etc.)	2	
43	Food handlers are equipped with suitable aprons, gloves, headgear, etc. wherever necessary.	2	
Training & records keeping			
44	Internal/External audit of the system is done periodically. Check for records.	2	
45*	Food business has an effective consumer complaints redressal mechanism.	2	
46*	Food handlers have the necessary knowledge and skills, and are trained to handle food safely. Check for training records.	2	
47*	Appropriate documentation & records are available and retained for a period of one year.	2	
		Total	0

Your total score=_____/114

(Certain pointers may not be applicable to every vertical. For Instance, Quick Service Restaurants – do not follow the method of reheating, food portioning and they do not hold any food. So the point no. 25, 26, 27 is not applicable. Depending on the vertical and the nature of processing, use discretion to score)

Grading

☐   114-102 A+ Compliance Exemplary

☐   101-92ACompliance Satisfactory

☐   91- 82BNeeds Improvement

☐   <82 No grade Non-compliance

Approved Suppliers Record List

SNO	ITEM/MATERIAL NAME	SUPPLIER DETAIL			
		CONTACT PERSON	ADDRESS	CONTACT NUMBER	EMAIL ID

Customer Complaint Record

Product complaints are an important indicator of possible deficiencies of the preventive food safety control systems and/or pre-requisite programs. The FBO should develop and implement written procedures to handle product complaints. These should identify and trace the person or people responsible for receiving, evaluating, categorizing, investigating and addressing complaints.

SNO	DATE	TIME	ORDER NO.	FOOD ORDERED	NAME OF THE CUSTOMER	NUMBER OF THE CUSTOMER	CUSTOMER COMPLAINT	ACTION TAKEN	REASON

References

More information and detailed explanations, which have been left out of this book for the sake of crispness and brevity, can be obtained through the links given below.

1. **www. fssai. gov. in**
2. (Food Safety Handbook by Dr. Pasupathy) **https://www. amazon.in/Food-Safety-Hand-Hospitality-Industry/dp/8189 275453 - By Dr. Pasupathy**

Food Safety Display Board

3. **https://archive. fssai. gov. in/home/safe-food-practices/ food-safety-display-boards. html**

Food Licensing and Registration and FoSCoS(Food Safety and Compliance System)

4. **https://foodlicensing. fssai. gov. in/index. aspx**
5. **https://fssai. gov. in/cms/standardsfaq. php**

6. https://www. fssai. gov. in/cms/food-safety-and-standards-regulations. php
7. https://www. fssai. gov. in/upload/uploadfiles/files/Contaminants_Regulations. pdf

Food Labelling and Packaging

8. https://www. fssai. gov. in/upload/uploadfiles/files/Packaging_Labelling_Regulations. pdf

Water Purification System

https://www. diesel-plus. com/the-seven-steps-of-the-water-purification-process/https://www.uwhealth.org/news/dr-jacqueline-gerhart-theres-good-and-bad-to-using-reverse-osmosis-water-systems/36710#:~:text=However%2C%20there%20are%20disadvantages., removed%2C%20depending%20on%20your%20system.

Hygiene Rating Checklist and FSSAI Testing Parameters

https://fssai. gov. in/hygieneRating/home

www.ingramcontent.com/pod-product-compliance
Lightning Source LLC
Chambersburg PA
CBHW030659220526
45463CB00005B/1839